GROWING AND EATING SUSTAINABLY

GROWING AND EATING SUSTAINABLY

AGROECOLOGY IN ACTION

DANA JAMES & EVAN BOWNESS

With contributors: Natal João Magnanti,
Fernando do Espírito Santo, Isadora Leite
Escosteguy and Oscar José Rover,
Erika Sagae, and Charles (Bagé) Lamb

Fernwood Publishing
Halifax & Winnipeg

Editing: Amber Riaz
Text design: Brenda Conroy
Cover design: John van der Woude
Printed and bound in Canada

Published by Fernwood Publishing
32 Oceanvista Lane, Black Point, Nova Scotia, B0J 1B0
and 748 Broadway Avenue, Winnipeg, Manitoba, R3G 0X3
www.fernwoodpublishing.ca

Fernwood Publishing Company Limited gratefully acknowledges the financial support of
the Government of Canada, the Canada Council for the Arts, the Manitoba Department
of Culture, Heritage and Tourism under the Manitoba Publishers Marketing Assistance
Program and the Province of Manitoba, through the Book Publishing Tax Credit, for our
publishing program. We are pleased to work in partnership with the Province of Nova Scotia
to develop and promote our creative industries for the benefit of all Nova Scotians.

Library and Archives Canada Cataloguing in Publication

Title: Growing and eating sustainably: agroecology in action / by Dana James and Evan Bowness.
Names: James, Dana (Scholar), author. | Bowness, Evan, author.
Description: Includes bibliographical references and index.
Identifiers: Canadiana (print) 20210262559 | Canadiana (ebook) 20210262621 | ISBN 9781773634821
(softcover) | ISBN 9781773635101 (EPUB) | ISBN 9781773635002 (PDF)
Subjects: LCSH: Agricultural ecology—Brazil. | LCSH: Sustainable agriculture—Brazil.
| LCSH: Food—Social aspects—Brazil.
Classification: LCC S475.B72 J36 2021 | DDC 338.10981—dc23

CONTENTS

ACRONYMS

AGRECO	Associação dos Agricultores Ecológicos das Encostas da Serra Geral (Association of Ecological Farmers of the Encostas da Serra Geral)
ANA	Articulação Nacional de Agroecologia (National Agroecology Alliance)
CAFO	concentrated animal feeding operations
CCR	Células de Consumidores Responsáveis (Responsible Consumer Cells)
CEPAGRO	Centro de Estudos e Promoção da Agricultura de Grupo (Centre for the Study and Promotion of Collective Agriculture)
CONSEA	Conselho Nacional de Segurança Alimentar e Nutricional (National Council on Food and Nutritional Security)
CSA	community-supported agriculture
EPAGRI	Empresa de Pesquisa Agropecuária e Extensão Rural de Santa Catarina (Company of Agricultural Research and Rural Extension of Santa Catarina)
FAO	Food and Agriculture Organization of the United Nations
FOM	mixed ombrophilous forest
FUNAI	Fundação Nacional do Índio (National Indigenous Foundation)
GHG	greenhouse gas
HHPS	highly hazardous pesticides
HLPE	High-Level Panel of Experts on Food Security and Nutrition
INCRA	Instituto Nacional de Colonização e Reforma Agrária (Institute for Colonization and Agrarian Reform)
IPM	integrated pest management
LVC	La Vía Campesina
MAB	Movimento dos Atingidos por Barragens (The Movement of People Affected by Dams)
MAPA	Ministério da Agricultura, Pecuária e Abastecimento (Ministry of Agriculture, Livestock, and Supply)
MMC	Movimento de Mulheres Camponesas (Rural Women's Movement)
MST	Movimento dos Trabalhadores Rurais Sem Terra (Landless Rural Workers' Movement)
NGO	non-governmental organization
NTFP	non-timber forest products
PACUCA	Parque Cultural do Campeche
PGS	participatory guarantee systems
PNAE	Programa Nacional de Alimentação Escolar (National School Feeding Program)
PSC	Planalto Serrano Catarinense (Santa Catarina plateau)
UBC	University of British Columbia

ACKNOWLEDGEMENTS

First, we are most grateful to the growers, researchers, and community organizers who worked with us during this project and so generously and patiently shared their time, experiences, and delicious food with us — two researchers from a foreign university. To those on-the-ground experts — we hope that this book honours your stories and the important work that you do, day in and day out. *A luta continua.*

We extend our deepest gratitude to the Centre for the Study and Promotion of Collective Agriculture (o Centro de Estudos e Promoção da Agricultura de Grupo, CEPAGRO), a non-governmental organization (NGO) based in Santa Catarina, which has been both a partner in the research and a home base for us in Brazil. We are forever appreciative of CEPAGRO's ongoing collaboration, the shared learning, and its members' warm hospitality. We are similarly grateful to Natal João Magnanti and Carol Couto Waltrich of Centro Vianei, who were equally instrumental in shaping and carrying out this project. We thank Ademir Cazella and a Programa de Pós-Graduação em Agroecossistemas at the Federal University of Santa Catarina, who were the sponsors of our stays in Brazil, as well as Adinor Capellesso of the Federal Institute of Santa Catarina and Juliana Luiz for their support in facilitating portions of the fieldwork. Most of the visits[1] that we made to farms, markets, protests, and other events were the result of connections made through our relationships with these wonderful people and organizations (a number of whom also feature as contributors throughout this book).

We thank our PhD supervisor, Hannah Wittman, for her support of this project and her dedication to community-based research, as well as the team at Fernwood — Bev Rach for wrangling the production process, the designers, our copyeditor Amber Riaz, and especially our editor Wayne Antony for his unwavering encouragement, enthusiasm for, and belief in this book. We extend our gratitude to the two anonymous reviewers who provided kind, generous, and constructive feedback on this manuscript. Lastly, we are thankful for the direct funding support provided to this project through the University of British Columbia's Public Scholars Initiative, Mitacs International, and the Social Sciences and Humanities Research Council of Canada, and we gratefully acknowledge the land on which this research took place — the territories of the Guaraní/Mbyá, Kaingang, and Laklanõ peoples.

WHO IS THIS BOOK FOR?

This book is for people who want to learn about agroecology — about the concepts, themes, key writings, and grassroots struggles from which it has emerged to become an internationally recognized paradigm for building more sustainable and just food systems. It will be most useful to those who are generally interested in agroecology, food sovereignty, sustainable food systems, and similar topics but are still relatively new to them.

There are many excellent resources on agroecology and related topics, but this book aims to do something a little different in two ways: First, while this is an introduction to agroecology and "agroecological transitions," it is presented through stories comprised of vignettes and photos. Agroecology is a way of reorganizing food and agricultural systems, but it's also a way of life for people. And sometimes, when learning about such concepts and social issues, the real people doing the work on the ground can get lost in academic abstractions. We think that our use of stories and photographs helps to bring these ideas — and the people promoting them — to life in a more tangible way.

Second, this book prioritizes the voices and experiences of those working at the forefront of the agroecology movement. Academic theorizations take a back seat. We do draw on agroecological scholarship and critical food-systems analysis, but the focus is on making concepts relatable and understandable. This makes for a book that (we hope!) amplifies the work of those who so generously shared their stories with us, while also introducing the broader academic foundations of agroecology.

Since we as authors are accountable to the agroecological farmers, activists, policymakers, and movements that are working toward more equitable and sustainable food systems, we wrote this book with community groups and people working on these issues in mind. For us, this book facilitates what in the agroecology movement is called a *diálogo de saberes* ("dialogue of knowledges").[1] The *diálogo de saberes* refers to the flow and exchange of ideas and experiences across diverse cultural contexts. Central to agroecology is the sharing of knowledge from one local experience to another through farmer–grower networks and through larger social networks that include not only growers but also eaters, workers, researchers, activists, and organizers. This book provides one pathway through which food-systems students and activists in Canada and other English-speaking countries, particularly those in the Global

North, can learn from the real-life efforts of those working toward more just and sustainable food futures in one of the epicentres of the global agroecology movement: Brazil.[2] Brazil has a rich history of social movements that have contributed greatly to the development of agroecology in theory and in practice — it is where some of the most vibrant examples of agroecology can be found. Our intention is to celebrate and share knowledge from the agroecology movement in Brazil so that scholar-activists in North America/Turtle Island[3] can learn from their valuable experiences. To this end, some of the stories in this book are written by Brazilian colleagues to incorporate their expertise and in-depth knowledge of agroecology directly.[4]

Growing and Eating Sustainably both shows and tells how agroecological transitions unfold. While rooted in experiences and examples from Brazil, the stories reflect responses to issues that are widespread in the globalized industrial food system, which has contributed to multiple socioecological crises, including climate change, soil and water degradation, and social inequities. We hope you can draw inspiration from these stories to push for a change in food systems in your own communities.

FOREWORD

When I was a child growing up on a large farm and ranch in the Pacific Northwest of the United States, my first-hand experience of "growing and eating sustainably" seemed like just a natural way of life. We grew most of our own food and worked many chores, including taking care of animals, "picking rock" out of the fields, and getting up at 3:00 a.m. to pull invasive weeds from wheat seed crops. As I grew into my teenage years, my duties expanded to include bookkeeping for the farm, and I began to understand the serious impact of commodity price fluctuations — and unexpected summer hailstorms — on my family's livelihood. Money was scarce and I started taking extra work in town to prepare for getting off the farm as fast as I could. I have now come full circle and study the global food system, working with community and farmer organizations across the world to identify pathways for bridging the trade-offs and tensions between livelihoods, family well-being, job quality, environmental sustainability, and food security. Along with my students — including the authors of this volume, Dana James and Evan Bowness — I work to understand the challenges posed by the transformation from diverse, place-based food systems based on close relationships between farmers, eaters, and the natural environment, to a global food system that is now based on the flow of a few commodity crops largely controlled by multinational corporations. This transformation has contributed to a public health crisis through the "nutrition transition," leading to high levels of diet-related disease; climate and biodiversity crises; and the exploitation of farmers and farm workers.

In response to those challenges, agroecological transitions present a bright pathway toward more sustainable, equitable, and just food systems. Now recognized globally as an approach to agriculture that seeks to balance the metabolism between society and nature, agroecological approaches build on traditional and Indigenous knowledge and have proven to be adaptive in the face of climate change. Agroecology is also rapidly entering the policy, educational, and technical spaces, including the Food and Agriculture Organization of the United Nations, which recognizes agroecology as a rights- and equity-based approach that can support the participation of youth, women, and other marginalized social groups to achieve viable and thriving livelihoods and contribute to the restoration of working land-scapes across the globe.

The stories and photos in this volume beautifully illustrate how this can be done. Based on their close research engagement with social movement actors in southern Brazil, Dana James and Evan Bowness provide a window of inspiration into the elements of agroecological "system redesign" linking growers and eaters to build sustainable and just food systems for our collective future.

— Hannah Wittman
June 2021

Chapter 1

INTRODUCING AGROECOLOGY AND FOOD-SYSTEMS TRANSITIONS

The COVID-19 pandemic sent unprecedented shock waves through the global economy, threatening the foundations on which society depends for safety, security, and sustenance. Perhaps nowhere is this more visible than in our collective relationship to food. When travel and import bans were imposed due to COVID-19 and businesses were forced to stop operating, food supply chains were disrupted. Consumers panicked, as they fought over seemingly scarce products in grocery stores. Frontline food and farm workers were declared essential while also being forced to work in confined spaces at increased risk of contracting SARS-CoV-2, the virus that causes COVID-19. Tens of millions of people (estimates range between 83 and 150 million globally) have been driven into conditions of acute hunger due to a loss in livelihoods, incomes, and access to food[1] — in addition to the 135 million people who were already living with crisis-level hunger prior to the pandemic.[2]

These critical issues made headlines daily across the globe and highlighted the vulnerabilities of the modern *food system*. When we use the term "food system" (or "food systems"), we are referring to all of the institutions and people involved in producing, processing, transporting, selling, consuming, recycling, or otherwise managing the food upon which our societies depend. Food systems also include the environmental, social, economic, and political factors that shape these institutions and processes. Take agriculture, for instance. As a fundamental component of the broader food system (and as a system itself), agriculture involves farmers and workers who produce food. This process requires inputs — like seeds, and those farmers' and workers' labour — and is shaped by broader conditions, including biophysical conditions such as weather and climate, topography, and soil type, as well as social, economic, and political conditions, including human values, market access, and agricultural policy.

The contemporary global food system is often described as "industrial" because it can be characterized by some key features that emerged in full force during the Industrial Revolution — the period of time (roughly the mid-1700s to mid-1800s) marked by technological developments that allowed fossil fuels, particularly coal, to be burned to harness energy at a scale never before witnessed. So, what are some of these key features of industrialization?

First, industrialization remains a very energy-intensive process. An enormous amount of energy is used today to produce, transport, process, and distribute food, with estimates that the food sector is responsible for 13 to 30 percent of energy consumption globally.[3] This includes, for example, the fact that industrial agriculture is heavily dependent upon agrichemicals, including synthetic fertilizers and pesticides. Producing these agrichemicals requires fossil energy inputs, with around 10 to 15 calories of fossil energy needed to produce 1 calorie of food. Yet despite all of the energy that goes into the industrial food system, around 30 percent of all food — and therefore, the energy and resources that were used to produce it — ends up being lost or wasted along the path from farm to fork due to factors like inadequate storage and spoilage.[4]

Second, industrialization includes and refers to certain processes, such as specialization (focusing specifically on doing or producing one thing) and homogenization (making elements similar to one another, or standardized and uniform). In agriculture, specialization and homogenization — coupled with access to fossil-fuel-based mechanization — have fuelled a tendency to produce food in large-scale monocultures (of one type of crop or animal), contributing to "economies of scale" (lowering the cost per unit of production as a result of efficiencies gained through mass production). In this way, industrialization created new possibilities for transforming nature at a tremendous scale by replacing human and animal labour with fossil-fuel-based technologies or otherwise reducing labour inputs.

Third, the industrial food system is also embedded within the larger neoliberal and global capitalist economy, which means that it treats food as a commodity to be produced and exchanged in a "free market," where the primary motivation is the creation of private profit. Neoliberalism as a concept and a political doctrine entails a shift away from state-led governance of social programming and markets through a devolution of power to the private sector. In the contemporary neoliberal food economy, the vast majority of profits are captured by a network of agrifood corporations (for example, farm input suppliers, food manufacturing conglomerates, and retail chains) that have become increasingly globalized (meaning that they operate across national borders). These corporations — or transnational or multinational corporations as they are often called — are able to accrue enormous profits because they have captured control of the market: for example, only four firms — Corteva, Bayer, BASF, and ChemChina/Syngenta — control 65 percent of the global agrichemical market; all of these firms are also major players in the seed sector.[5] Another example of corporate concentration in the food system is that of what turkey producers face. Those producers reliant upon animal genetics companies for artificial insemination virtually have only two "choices" available to them because "only two firms control 99 percent of turkey genetics."[6] As a result, the industrial food system is dominated by just a few corporations that wield an

A "McDonaldized" grocery store in Florianópolis, Santa Catarina, Brazil. Everything is ordered, uniform, and convenient.

incredible amount of power over farmers, workers, and eaters. These corporations are able to put pressure on governments to relax regulations that moderate their ability to accumulate profits, including those that are intended to protect the environment and enforce standards for working conditions.[7]

There are a variety of ways to describe how logics of industrialization and neoliberal capitalism have permeated the food system and our everyday lives. George Ritzer came up with the term "McDonaldization" to refer to how people and institutions today are increasingly characterized by features that are most evident at fast food chains: control, calculability, efficiency, and predictability.[8]

Ritzer's analysis was based on the work of a classical sociologist, Max Weber, who argued that the determining force that shaped modern society was *rationalization*.[9] While the common-sense use of the term rationalization means "to justify" or "to explain" one's actions, sociologists use the term in a specific way. Rationalization describes a pattern where people and societies become characterized by a preoccupation with finding technologies and forms of social organization that allow for more precisely controlling, systematizing, and extracting value from the world, in pursuit of better lives for people (at least theoretically). This tendency became pervasive during the Industrial Revolution and resulted in radical changes to nature and all aspects of society.

IS THE INDUSTRIAL FOOD SYSTEM SUSTAINABLE?

We've established that the global food system currently relies on energy-intensive technologies and industrial processes to produce food, and is largely controlled by highly concentrated and powerful agrifood corporations that distribute food commodities at a global scale. So, what are the implications of this? On the one hand, it is thanks to the industrial food system that we see an incredible selection of cheap food on the shelves at a grocery store or on the menu at a restaurant. In Canada and the United States, for example, people on average now spend only about 5 to 10 percent of their income on food — a historic low and much lower than in many other countries around the world. And indeed, we are often told by the agrifood corporations that control so much of the food system that they play a key role in "feeding the world."

However, despite the "efficiencies" of the industrial food system and the seemingly countless options we now have at the store, there is still persistent hunger around the world, including in high-income countries like Canada and the United States. So, while globally there is now more than enough food to feed the world, the major bottleneck in realizing food security (or stable and regular access to food) for the world's approximately two billion food insecure people[10] is less a problem of yield and production and more about the inequitable distribution of and access to food as a result of poverty, wealth inequality, and inadequate infrastructure and social programming (including safety nets and social welfare). In other words, the reason we have persistent hunger is not because there is not enough food but because the capitalist market restricts access to it.

Also critical to this discussion is the fact that these supposedly "cheap" foods are not really all that cheap — there are many hidden costs to this "efficient" system that need to be taken into account. At first glance, the relatively low prices of the bewildering selection of foods available at the market seem to benefit us as consumers, but at closer examination, it becomes clear that this is only because we are not paying the true cost of our food up front. However, we do pay for it later — cheap foods (typically featuring a roster of corn, wheat, and soy derivatives) have contributed to low-quality, highly processed diets that have made society's healthcare costs skyrocket. And, ironically, what appears to be a diversity of options at the grocery store masks the fact that there has been a steep decline in crop and animal diversity globally.[11] As a result of this declining biodiversity, we have also lost many of the cultural traditions that were developed around local plant and animal varieties. Put another way, the world is losing "biocultural heritage," and the culprit is largely industrial food production. In addition to the loss of diversity, other environmental effects of industrial agriculture include deforestation (when trees are cleared to make space to grow/raise more food) and pollution (especially when agrichemicals make their way into surrounding ecosystems). It is increasingly clear that these environmental damages are contributing to ecological catastrophes at a global scale, including mass extinction and climate change, which in turn threaten the very foundations upon which agriculture depends. And these are only some of the social and environmental problems associated with industrial agriculture. So, ultimately, the environment and our communities do pay the costs (otherwise known as "negative externalities") of artificially cheap food many times over — but the large agrifood companies that are responsible for the damage too often do not.[12]

IS THE INDUSTRIAL FOOD SYSTEM RESILIENT?

As we previously mentioned, the globalized and industrialized food system is deeply intertwined with other systems, such as the energy system (which largely involves the production, trade, and consumption of fossil fuels) and the economic system (which provides financial resources, or capital, to the food system). Because of these interdependencies, disruptions to any one system or component of a system can have ripple effects that pose risks to environmental sustainability, economic and political stability, and human health and well-being. Because of the industrial food system's dependency on other unsustainable systems and because there is a lack of redundancy in the system due to corporate concentration and control over food supply chains, we can generally say that the food system is not very resilient. "Resilience" refers to the capacity of a system — in this case, the food system — to adapt to shocks and stressors, and an associated ability to continue functioning — in this case, by producing and distributing healthy foods — in the face of those shocks and stressors.

So, while some problems may not seem directly related to food — like changes in oil prices or economic recessions, for example — there are many examples of how disruptions to one of these systems has contributed to disruptions in another. At a global scale, the COVID-19 pandemic was one reminder of this; another was the food price crisis of 2007–2008, when food prices — particularly of staples such as rice, wheat, and maize — sharply increased. The price spike was triggered by a confluence of factors, including financial speculation, rising oil prices, an expanding biofuel market, environmental events such as droughts, and protectionist food policies (among others).[13] And in May 2018, another example of a shock occurred in Brazil — this time at the national level. As a country, Brazil is highly dependent on trucking: almost 70 percent of goods within Brazil, including food, materials, and fuel, are moved by truck. And, of course, truck drivers are dependent upon affordable and accessible diesel fuel. For a long time, Brazil's national government had set oil price measures that subsidized oil and gas. But in 2016, the state-owned oil company, Petrobras, ended these measures in order to bring domestic oil prices more in line with the international market.[14] As a result, diesel prices in Brazil climbed, squeezing truck drivers' already small margins, which, in part, led them to go on strike in 2018. As a result of the strike, supermarket shelves went empty, tonnes of perishable produce were lost, and millions of farm animals died of starvation or had to be slaughtered prematurely. Many cities ended up facing major food, water, and health supply shortages.

Just as with COVID-19, the disruption caused by the strike made visible the fragility of Brazil's national food system. Paulo Petersen, an international leader in sustainable food scholarship and policy advocacy in Brazil asserts:

> [The trucking] crisis revealed the degree of vulnerability of [our current] model. A few days of a truck drivers' strike were enough for the system to collapse. This is a demonstration of the infeasibility of a food system that depends on transport at great distances and that drives territories to import more of what they consume and export more of what they produce. Whether for environmental, energy, or economic reasons, this pattern is unsustainable because it is structurally dependent on the consumption of fossil fuels.[15]

These disruptions are a result of how the industrial food system is organized. Because it is highly dependent on other unsustainable systems, the food system is just as vulnerable to threats to those systems. In addition, because the industrial food system lacks redundancy and diversity, it is less resilient and at potentially greater risk of system collapse.[16] In today's world, pandemics and other unfolding crises (such as climate change) pose global-scale threats to the food system as we know it. Considering all of this, it is essential that the food system be reorganized in a way that maximizes resilience. This brings us to an alternative approach based on diversity — an approach known as "agroecology."

ENVISIONING AGROECOLOGY

Agroecology, or the design and management of agrifood systems according to ecological and social justice principles, emerged "to respond to the mounting problems resulting from an increasingly globalized and industrialized agri-food system."[17] Agroecological scientists were originally interested in seeing how insights from ecology could be used to improve farming systems; if growers could model their farms on ecological systems and work with rather than against nature, they could become more sustainable and resilient in the long run. But beyond being motivated by ecological sustainability, peasant farmers from the Global South have long been at the forefront of advocating for agroecology as part of broader demands for "food sovereignty," or the rights of people to produce food and define and control their own food systems.[18] While ecologically based farming practices have the potential to improve agricultural sustainability across farms of various sizes and production systems, the key role that agrarian movements have played in promoting agroecology has led to it often being associated with the "traditional" farming sector (small-scale, peasant, and Indigenous agriculture), in large part because traditional farming practices are rooted in deep, place-based ecological knowledge and experiences. In addition, the promotion of small-scale farming is grounded in concerns about social justice, as many smallholders have been displaced, outcompeted, and marginalized as a result of neoliberal agrifood policy, which has favoured large landowners and corporations and contributed to the consolidation of land and power in the agrifood sector. Social justice — or the fair distribution of opportunities, benefits, and risks to different social groups along intersecting lines of race, gender, class, and other social markers of identity — is, therefore, a key concept in agroecology.

These various threads have led to agroecology being commonly described as a science, a practice, and a social movement.[19] It is a science because it is rooted in ecological approaches to studying and understanding agricultural systems — agroecology is a way of thinking holistically about the relationships between soil, plants, animals, and their natural contexts and for conducting research on how to harmonize agricultural production with ecological processes. One of the key academic texts[20] on agroecology describes it as "participatory" (in that it engages and includes real people and their experiences), "transdisciplinary" (in that it transcends academic disciplines and prioritizes collaborations across sectors), and "action-oriented" (in that the knowledge produced through agroecological research is first and foremost practical, focused on problems and solutions). While we do not focus deeply on describing or advancing the science of agroecology, we have taken a scientific approach to agroecology (valuing participation, transdisciplinarity, and action-oriented research) in the creation of this project.

Beyond being a science, agroecology can also be considered a practice because it refers to the things that people do to make the world "more agroecological" — both in terms of farming methods but also in terms of social relations. In contrast to an industrial food system, agroecological food systems translate ecological principles (for example, diversification and the recycling of nutrients and biomass) into agricultural management practices (for example, intercropping and composting) in order to enjoy and enhance ecosystem services, or the services provided to people by nature. An agroecological food system also incorporates social justice principles (for instance, the right to dignified work) and puts them into practice (for example, by ensuring farmers and farm workers are fairly compensated).

Agroecology also refers to a social movement, or a collection of people who organize outside of formal political channels to pursue (or resist) social change. We refer to the groups of people demanding a food system based on agroecology as the "agroecology movement." This movement is global in scope and is made up of many smaller organizations, institutions, and communities that collectively mobilize in pursuit of progressive social, political, economic, and environmental changes in the food system. Broadly, the agroecology movement aims to challenge dominant and inequitable power relations by connecting with and nurturing those at the heart of the food system — growers, workers, eaters, and the land. As such, transitioning from an industrial food system toward an agroecological one requires a radical shift in our institutions, relationships, and values.[21] This will necessarily entail large-scale changes to how we grow, process, distribute, consume, and dispose of food.

Our aim in this book is to envision the transition from industrial to agroecological food systems. We use the word "envision" for two reasons: first, we intend to not only introduce agroecology, but to also show what the agroecology movement in southern Brazil is doing on the ground. We use photos where possible, allowing a glimpse into the real experiences of those in the agroecology movement as they enact food-systems change and breathe life into the concept of agroecology.

Second, we bring this work into conversation with the work of late critical sociologist Erik Olin Wright, whose Envisioning Real Utopias project[22] involves proposing solutions to social problems that "embody emancipatory [or utopian] ideals" while remaining focused on the need to create "viable" or pragmatic institutional changes.[23] To that end, we highlight "cases of institutional innovations that embody in one way or another emancipatory alternatives to the dominant forms of social organization"[24] in the food system. Through this book, we provide a collection of place-based examples of agroecology in action that can help to envision alternatives to the industrial food system. These examples are presented as "vignettes" — introductions to people/groups that capture ethnographic or cultural details about their lives, using story as a means of explaining or exploring a broader theme or issue — that showcase different aspects of, and highlight key themes within, agroecological transitions. Hopefully, these vignettes can serve to build solidarity across borders and inspire food activists, scholars, farmers, and workers pushing for change in their own communities.

A few final notes are warranted on the visual element of "envisioning." Photography can provide valuable data for social science researchers. When visiting different actors in the agroecology movement in Brazil, we brought along cameras and a drone. We took photos during our visits (with consent) and shared them with the participants after. These photos are not professional works of art; they are real depictions of people living their lives — working, talking, eating, gathering, protesting, sharing, and learning. The photos that accompany the vignettes were all taken by the authors, who explained to the participants exactly why the photos were being taken (with the exception of photos taken in public places with many people present, such as a protest or event) and received their authorization to share them.

WHY BRAZIL?

Many farmers, food workers, researchers, community organizers, and activists across the world, particularly in the Global South, have been working to create more sustainable food systems by farming *with* nature and forming new social networks to support a transition to agroecology. We highlight some of those efforts in southern Brazil and show how agroecology can help mitigate or prevent the risks and harms associated with the industrial food system.

In many ways, Brazil can be considered a microcosm of the global food system: It is one of the most climatically, biologically, and socio-culturally diverse countries in the world, and is home to some of the most well-known and influential agrarian social movements that mobilize against a backdrop of deeply entrenched agribusiness interests. These two factions — radical food movements pushing for more sustainable and equitable food systems, and the agribusiness sector pushing for continued industrialization — are engaged in a struggle over the future of food in a country that is recognized as a globally important agricultural powerhouse. Many of the key elements of this struggle (the state-supported agribusiness sector on one side, and social movements on the other) are vibrant in Brazil, making it a strong case study from which to learn.

This is especially the case when it comes to the agroecology movement. One of the best-known radical food movements in Brazil is the Landless Rural Workers Movement (Movimento dos Trabalhadores Rurais Sem Terra, MST), which was a founding member of the international peasant organization La Vía Campesina (LVC), the largest agrarian social movement in the world. Another is Rede Ecovida, a decentralized network of around 4,000 farm families that has been operating in southern Brazil for more than twenty years. Rede Ecovida is known as one of the world's first "participatory guarantee systems," meaning that the members of the network certify one another as agroecological "based on active participation of stakeholders … built on a foundation of trust, social networks and knowledge exchange."[25] The south of Brazil is also home to a community group by the name of CEPAGRO, based in Florianópolis, Santa Catarina, which is a member organization of Rede Ecovida. CEPAGRO was instrumental in connecting us with the people and topics covered in this book, and several organizers and researchers within CEPAGRO's network contributed stories to this project. Due to the visibility and success of groups like Rede Ecovida and the MST, as well as the networking that happens at more local levels through organizations like CEPAGRO, southern Brazil has become known as a promising place for agroecology. Food movements in the Global North and other parts of the world could greatly benefit from learning more about the agroecological initiatives taking place in Brazil.

Brazil is also an important place to consider the barriers to food-systems transitions. The agriculture sector is economically important for Brazil in a number of ways. About 9 percent of Brazil's labour force works in agriculture.[26] Soy, raw sugar, poultry, and beef are among Brazil's biggest exports (soybeans alone represent 14 percent of all Brazilian exports in terms of monetary value),[27] and Brazil is the world's largest importer and consumer of pesticides and fertilizers. Brazilian agribusinesses are also dominant players in the global food economy; for example, the Brazilian company JBS is the largest beef producer in the world.[28] However, while agriculture is important to the Brazilian economy, it is also a driver of major environmental problems, such as deforestation and biodiversity loss. For example, more than 50 percent of the biodiversity hotspot known as the Brazilian Cerrado (a savanna ecosystem) has been converted into crop and pasture land, particularly for large-scale soybean plantations.[29] This tension between the economic importance of agriculture and its environmental effects makes the transition to sustainable agrifood systems politically contentious, because such a transition threatens powerful economic and political interests. Despite this larger policy environment that still heavily favours agribusiness and industrial agriculture, there is a lot to learn from grassroots movements in this key frontier in the struggle for sustainable and just food.

AGROECOLOGICAL TRANSITIONS

So far, we have been referring to the industrial food system and agroecological food systems as if there is a binary. While doing so can be useful to draw out the differences between these two approaches when it comes to growing, distributing, and consuming food, the reality is not so stark. Rather, these two systems can be viewed as ends of a spectrum, and our current food system(s) fall somewhere on that spectrum. Even the global "industrial food system" to which we have been referring is not entirely industrial; within this dominant system we still see lots of variability — think of your local organic farmers, or the fair trade movement, or Indigenous food trading practices. What we're interested in exploring is the gradient between industrial (often referred to elsewhere as "conventional") and agroecological farming, and how more industrial farms — and the industrial food system in general — can transition toward agroecology.

One of the best models for thinking about and understanding the concept of agroecological transitions is Stephen Gliessman's five-step framework for assessing food-systems change.[30] Gliessman classifies systems in transition according to five levels, where transitions across Levels 1 to 3 are mostly applied at the level of agroecosystems (encompassing the relationships between farmers, plants, animals, and inputs on farms), and Level 4 is at the level of regional food systems. Changes at these levels lead to an entirely transformed global food system at Level 5.[31] An overview of these levels follows:

- Level 1: "Increase the efficiency of industrial and conventional practices in order to reduce the use and consumption of costly, scarce, or environmentally damaging inputs."
- Level 2: "Substitute alternative practices for industrial/conventional inputs and practices."
- Level 3: "Redesign the agroecosystem so that it functions on the basis of a new set of ecological processes."
- Level 4: "Re-establish a more direct connection between those who grow our food and those who consume it."
- Level 5: "On the foundation created by the sustainable farm-scale agroecosystems achieved at Level 3, and the new relationships of sustainability of Level 4, build a new global food system, based on equity, participation, democracy, and justice, that is not only sustainable but helps restore and protect earth's life support systems upon which we all depend."

These levels are meant to draw our attention to how a transition to agroecology from an industrial food system is a process that takes place on specific farms, across landscapes, and throughout the food system, including in policy fora, in cities, in kitchens, and on individuals' plates. It is also important to note that while Gleissman's framework implies a linear shift from Level 1 toward Level 5, transitions are often nonlinear. More often than not, they are dynamic processes that involve trial and error, experimentation, and shifts back and forth along the spectrum.

With this caveat in mind, we have organized the stories in this book loosely in tandem with Gliessman's model. The history and problems of the industrial food system demonstrate why the world needs agroecology and point to some of the practices that are to be reduced in Level 1 and substituted in Level 2. Showing where agroecological food comes from, with a major focus on agroecological food production in rural areas corresponds roughly with Levels 2 and 3. Building new relationships in the food system, both in and between the city and the countryside, corresponds roughly to Levels 4 and 5. While organized according to Gliessman's framework, all of the stories featured here are unfolding at the same time, again illustrating how context-specific initiatives contribute to nonlinear transitions toward agroecology at larger scales.

This book is organized around a few key concepts. The food system encompasses all of the processes, resources, technologies, people, and institutions involved in growing, harvesting, storing, transporting, processing, distributing, consuming, wasting, and recycling food. The industrial food system relies on fossil fuel-based industrial processes and technologies, including agrichemical inputs like synthetic fertilizers and pesticides, to produce food at a massive scale. The industrial food system is environmentally unsustainable since it depends on finite resources (like fossil fuels), results in high levels of pollution, and reduces biodiversity. This system is also economically and socially unsustainable, because large-scale farms, retailers, and neoliberal policies (like deregulation and free trade) have displaced many farmers and rural workers and undermined their right to live on the land and produce food with dignity. The agrifood corporations and industrialized states that benefit from this system at the expense of others rely on a "feed the world" narrative to justify and maintain their role within the global food system. Yet, this claim belies the fact that there is already more than enough food in the world; the problem is that many people do not have access to it, primarily because of a lack of income, inadequate social safety nets, and the globally uneven distribution of food and power.[32] In the words of renowned economist Amartya Sen, "the problem of nourishment … in fact, belong[s] to political economy and to political science. There is, indeed, no such thing as an apolitical food problem."[33]

The problems associated with the industrial food system shine a light on the need to transition to alternatives. In general terms, a transition simply refers to a change from one state to another. But this raises some questions: what is changing, how is it changing, and what is it becoming? It is no longer radical to argue that the industrial food system is harmful to people and the planet. Therefore, what is needed is a large-scale shift from the industrial food system to more place-based food systems that respect planetary boundaries and planetary health;[34] in other words, food systems that are based in the science, practice, and social movement of agroecology. In Brazil, farmers and organizers articulate agroecology as encompassing "a way of life" guided by ethics of respect and care that disrupts the status quo. This stands counter to the industrial food system, which takes a production-oriented approach to growing and distributing food (meaning that the focus is on producing or yielding more in pursuit of profit, to the detriment of other important functions and outcomes). Instead, agroecology requires us to think about the many relationships that make up the food system, recognizing the multiple benefits provided to humans by the food system *beyond* yield and profit — for example, dignified work, stewardship of crop and animal diversity, and resilience to shocks like natural disasters, social unrest, and pandemics.

Chapter 2

THE INDUSTRIAL FOOD SYSTEM
Contradictions and Crises

In this chapter, we look more deeply at the industrial food system — its origins and the problems it generates — which casts yet more doubt on the conventional wisdom that industrial agriculture is the best way to "feed the world." Even though it is clear that a new system for growing and eating food is urgently needed, there are deeply entrenched historical and ongoing barriers that inhibit the transition to agroecological food systems.

A BRIEF OVERVIEW OF THE "GREEN REVOLUTION"

It is important to contextualize the origins of the industrial food system with some of the influential population and economic theories that have circulated over the past two hundred plus years. One of the most significant of these came from an economist named Thomas Malthus in the late 1700s. Malthus theorized that without proactive population control, exponential population growth would far outpace the global capacity to produce food, leading to famine and war that would bring the global population back in line with the planet's food-producing capacity.[1] During Malthus's time, the global population was still less than one billion people. Fast forward to the 1950s, and that number climbed to three billion[2] thanks to major gains in medicine and public health, which led to lower death rates and longer life expectancies. Yet, while the global population was growing, the availability of farmland was decreasing — seemingly lending weight to Malthus's ominous prediction.[3]

There are a number of problems with Malthusian population predictions that we will not get into here, but suffice it to say that the population crash that Malthus predicted never came to pass. One key reason for his failed prediction was the "technological leaps" in agricultural development that resulted from rationalization. For example, the invention of the Haber-Bosch process in the early twentieth century opened the door to industrial-scale production of synthetic ammonia for agricultural fertilizers. This invention allowed farmers to overcome nutrient depletion — particularly nitrogen depletion, which is a key limiting factor for agricultural productivity. Prior to the invention of the Haber-Bosch process, there was no large-scale method for adding nitrogen back into the soil after crops were harvested, and so the practice of intensive agriculture would quickly exhaust soil fertility (and hence productivity). The Haber-Bosch process therefore made crop yields and production possible at a scale previously unimaginable.

Other technologies that were important for increasing the global capacity to produce food through industrial agriculture were developed during what is known as the Green Revolution, a period corresponding roughly to the mid-1950s through to the mid-1970s that led to new high-yielding varieties of staple crops like wheat, maize, and rice. The Green Revolution combined high investments in the research and development of synthetic fertilizers and pesticides, irrigation, and mechanization with an innovative approach to plant breeding developed by Norman Borlaug, a scientist who is often referred to as the father of the Green Revolution. This new approach was called *shuttle breeding*, a strategy where the seeds selected from the plant breeding process are "shuttled" back and forth between different growing regions to speed up the process of developing new cultivars (intentionally bred plant varieties). Through shuttle breeding, scientists were able to select cultivars based on whether they possessed desired traits (for example, resistance to a specific disease) and ensure that these cultivars were capable of adapting to a wide array of soil, climate, and other conditions.[4] In large part due to this "package" of Green Revolution technologies, while the global population doubled between the mid-1960s to the mid-2000s, "the production of cereal crops tripled during this period, with only a 30 percent increase in land area cultivated"[5] — a remarkable feat.

The trajectory of food systems in Brazil mirrored many of these same patterns.[6] The Green Revolution approach to agricultural development was strongly taken up in Brazil in the 1960s and 1970s, when the country was still under a military dictatorship.[7] At the time, the Brazilian state invested heavily in research and extension in support of agricultural modernization, including through the National Rural Credit System, which provided a way to finance agricultural inputs for farmers.[8] In addition, the state-owned Brazilian Agricultural Research Corporation, Embrapa, was created in 1972 to further advance Green Revolution-inspired research and the spread of industrial agriculture.[9]

These efforts have "dramatically increased agricultural yields" in Brazil, particularly in frontier areas that were previously thought to be unsuitable for cultivation.[10] For example, the research of Embrapa was instrumental in opening up the Cerrado (the vast savanna region considered a biodiversity hotspot) to agriculture. Soils in the Cerrado are acidic and lacking in key nutrients that support soil fertility, so in general they are poorly suited to growing crops.[11] However, Green Revolution technologies like synthetic fertilizers and agricultural lime, in combination with Embrapa's plant breeding efforts, have transformed the region. Today, over one million square kilometres — more than half of the original Cerrado, or about 12.5 percent of Brazil's total land area — has been lost to large-scale, industrial plantations (principally of soybean grown for export, as well as maize and sugarcane) and extensive cattle grazing.[12]

This picture of a crop storage facility was taken in the western part of Santa Catarina. The text on the massive silos reads: "The man. The land. The technology. The union."

Beyond state-sponsored research, the Brazilian state also subsidized Green Revolution technologies and education, which provided an incentive for farmers to "modernize" their agricultural practices. Yet, these subsidies were aimed at supporting relatively large-scale farming operations, leaving many small farms unable to compete with larger farms that were better able to access these subsidized inputs and resources. Ultimately, many small-scale farmers were outcompeted, and they migrated to urban areas to look for jobs, fuelling the development of *favelas* (informal communities). Other landless peasants sought land by invading Indigenous reserves and, later, large unused rural estates, setting the stage for what would become the MST.[13] As the social tensions around these multiple layers of dispossession (or removal from the land) heightened, so did awareness of other negative externalities associated with industrial agriculture. One of the most prominent negative externalities in Brazil is the role of industrial agriculture in driving deforestation.[14] The main culprit of deforestation in the Brazilian Amazon, for example, is large-scale cattle ranching "with large- and medium-sized ranches accounting for about 70 percent of clearing activity."[15]

FEEDING THE WORLD?

Fast forward to today and, in terms of calories, there is already more than enough food to feed the world.[16] And yet, two billion people still do not have regular access to adequate food, with around 750 million of these people (around 10 percent of the global population) living in conditions of severe food insecurity.[17] Another two billion people experience malnutrition in the form of overweight or obesity, given the fact that the most affordable and convenient foods are typically the most processed and least nutritious.[18] This has led to what economist Raj Patel calls the paradox of "the stuffed and the starved."[19] More paradoxical still is that many of the same people who experience food insecurity and malnutrition actually depend on jobs in the agrifood sector to support themselves and their families, but these jobs are often precarious and poorly remunerated. Unfortunately, given the fact that food is treated as a commodity under capitalism, healthy food is accessible only to those who can afford it.

Of the abundance of foods produced around the world, 14 percent is lost (across stages of the food chain pre-retail/consumption) and another 17 percent is wasted (at the retail/consumption stage), which adds to the tragic paradox of global hunger.[20] Food loss and waste happen at various points in the food system: on farms (for instance, due to overproduction or damage), during distribution and processing (for instance, due to improper storage or refrigeration for perishables), and at the point of sale and consumption (for instance, due to large portions or confusion over date labels). Further contributing to these inefficiencies and inequities is the fact that land that could be used to grow crops for direct human consumption is instead used to grow industrial animal feed or livestock. While livestock contribute to nutrient cycling, play an important role in many cultures, and improve food security and nutrition in many parts of the world (particularly for small-scale farmers and pastoralists, as well as those living in marginal lands),[21] industrial livestock production — largely fuelled by affluent consumers' high demand for animal protein — has a large negative ecological and public health footprint. Put another way, high consumption of industrial animal products comes with negative externalities and an opportunity cost, because arable land that could be used to grow food directly for people is instead being used to produce industrial feed for livestock.

NEGATIVE EXTERNALITIES: UNDERSTANDING THE TRUE COST OF INDUSTRIAL FOOD SYSTEMS

The perverse health and environmental outcomes caused by the global food system are often not accounted for. Beyond the industrial food system leading to chronic diseases stemming from over- and under-nourishment, there are also health problems associated with exposure to agrichemicals and other forms of pollution as well as the growing threat of animal antibiotic resistance. Additionally, many scientists have documented the numerous negative effects on the environment caused by industrial agriculture, including water scarcity,[22] soil erosion,[23] and harm to sensitive ecosystems. Scientists have consistently warned that industrial agriculture is one of the major contributors to biodiversity loss and climate change — and that we must take drastic and immediate action to prevent further damage.[24] For example, it is estimated that 80 percent of deforestation globally between 2000 and 2010 could be attributed to agriculture,[25] and agriculture is responsible for 11 percent of the world's anthropogenic greenhouse gas (GHG) emissions (not accounting for emissions caused as a result of land-use changes due to agriculture, such as deforestation).[26] Yet there still hasn't been any major progress on halting the sixth mass extinction or the global climate crisis. And notably, given that industrial agriculture includes large-scale concentrated animal feeding operations (CAFOs) and relies on global trade, this system also creates conditions ripe for spreading pandemics.[27]

Some of these same negative externalities undermine industrial agriculture's capacity to continue to produce food in the first place. With CAFOs, for example, industrial agriculture's emphasis on control, efficiency, and calculability has led to immense numbers of animals being confined in tight spaces, with CAFOs often hosting tens of thousands of animals under a single roof. These animals can be highly genetically similar to one another — with few highly commercialized breeds and with animals bred from few production lines for the most profitable characteristics, such as rapid weight gain. (The animal genetics market itself is highly concentrated in the hands of two or three corporations, notably for turkeys, layer hens, broiler chickens, and pigs.[28]) This lack of genetic diversity, combined with stressful and often unsanitary conditions, makes farm animals in CAFOs increasingly vulnerable to diseases. Because housing many animals together in tight spaces increases the chance of disease spread, preventative animal pharmaceuticals — yet another highly concentrated sector, where eight firms control 80 percent of sales[29] — are required in an attempt to stop infections from wiping out entire animal operations. As a result, "73% of all antimicrobials sold on Earth are used in animals raised for food," contributing to the growing problem of antimicrobial resistance in both animals and humans and exacerbating the risk of infectious diseases.[30]

Another example of industrial agriculture's tendency to undermine its own conditions of existence has to do with the basic fact that — through natural selection — pests eventually develop resistance to chemical pesticides. Following the McDonaldized logics of efficiency and control, industrial agriculture relies on fields of monocultures. Planting rows of the same crop — and often, only that crop — in the same location season after season helps increase efficiency when it comes to planting and harvesting. But monoculture crop production lacks resilience in the same way that CAFOs undermine resilience — by increasing the risk of devastating pest outbreaks or diseases. The pests that manage to survive the agrichemical dosing reproduce, and in so doing, pass the traits that kept them alive on to their offspring. The next generation of pests, then, may require stronger chemicals or chemicals applied at greater volumes. The result is a dependence on greater and greater quantities of pesticides and herbicides or the development of more and more toxic agrichemicals to combat the more resistant pests and weeds — leading to what has been called "the pesticide treadmill."[31] This pattern is having disastrous effects, especially in terms of chemical run-off, where toxic chemicals make their way into waterways and can pose a serious risk to both human and environmental health.[32]

THE TOXICITY OF INDUSTRIAL AGRICULTURE

The toxic effects of agrichemicals are highly visible in Brazil, which has been the world's top consumer of pesticides since 2008, with sales estimated at around US$10 billion per year.[33] Worse yet, approximately half of the pesticides used in the country are classified as highly hazardous pesticides (HHPs), which the United Nations defines as "pesticides that are acknowledged to present particularly high levels of acute or chronic hazards to health or the environment according to internationally accepted classification systems."[34] This also makes Brazil the largest market for HHPs in the world. According to a recent investigative report, "the world's five biggest agrichemical companies — Syngenta, Bayer, BASF, Corteva, and FMC — accounted for four-fifths of all Brazil pesticide sales … and three-quarters of the country's highly hazardous pesticide sales."[35] These companies continue to sell HHPs in Brazil and elsewhere, despite the fact that these pesticides are banned in the countries where those same companies' headquarters are located.

While a complex array of factors interacts to affect human and environmental health, the body of evidence that documents the risks associated with pesticides is substantial. For example, neonicotinoids (the most popular class of insecticides in the world) have been linked to the steep decline of pollinator populations,[36] while exposure to glyphosate (the active agent used most widely for herbicides around the world) is connected to the increased risk of cancer.[37] These kinds of risks associated with HHPs, in combination with their widespread (over)use in Brazil, led the United Nations Special Rapporteur on human rights and hazardous substances and wastes to proclaim:

> The tremendous use of pesticides is resulting in grave impacts on human rights in Brazil. Food production and economic growth are not a legitimate excuse for these preventable violations and abuses. Victims rightly allege deaths, health problems, as well as cruel, inhuman and degrading treatment resulting from pesticide exposure. Environmental degradation, including water contamination and biodiversity loss including of bees are grave effects.[38]

Beyond the human rights abuses resulting from pesticide exposure, there are also reports of increasing violence related to the pesticide trade,[39] as well as attacks by agribusiness and landowners on Indigenous Peoples, Afro-Brazilians, landless peasants, and other traditional populations by aerially spraying communities and houses with agrotoxins.[40]

Despite the already shocking levels of pesticide availability and use in Brazil, the current Bolsonaro administration and the prior Temer administration have approved thousands of additional pesticides — 10 percent of which are banned elsewhere.[41] These approvals have occurred in tandem with the dismantling of environmental and human rights regulations and protections in Brazil. Bolsonaro's efforts to roll back such protections in the interest of agribusiness in Brazil culminated in the approval of updated Bill 6,299/2002, dubbed the "Poison Package" by many public health officials and critics. According to one scholar, the Poison Package "assumes the primacy of agribusiness's economic interests rather than defending health and the environment … [it] dismantles [the] wide legal framework and prevailing institutional structure in the country."[42] In addition, some have argued that the heavy dependency on pesticides developed by transnational agribusinesses has essentially transferred wealth out of Brazil's national coffers and into the pockets of foreign-owned corporations, at the expense of Brazilians' health and environmental well-being.[43]

In the south of Brazil, where the farmers featured in this book live and work, 63 percent of farms use agrotoxins.[44] This, by far, makes the south of Brazil the region with the highest proportion of households that use agrotoxins; the next closest is the southeast region, where that number is 28 percent.

SALETE AND ALUÍSIO: GETTING OFF THE PESTICIDE TREADMILL

The household of Dona Salete and Seu Aluísio used to be one such farming household in Brazil's south that relied on pesticides. Up until about a decade before we met them, they had been growing tobacco and spraying it with pesticides for thirty years (the commercial production of tobacco in Brazil is very agrichemical-intensive). This mode of production took a heavy toll on their health. In the words of Aluísio,

> I had been intoxicated from tobacco production. We worked in protective equipment, with that hot sun, in overall suits, masks, gloves, boots, everything that was needed. We'd finish, come home, take a shower, and I'd go to eat but instead I'd be vomiting, sick in bed with a headache. It was often like this.

They knew that they wanted to make a change to improve their family's health. And then they were approached by some agronomists with a potential market opportunity — to produce organic grapes, which the agronomists would then purchase. They decided to transition their whole property away from intensive tobacco production to a diversified agroecological farm that included organically grown grapes.

According to Aluísio,

> As soon as we transitioned we were already sure of our decision because immediately our health started to improve. I had been on medication, but stopped — stopped all

Seu Aluísio in his kitchen (left) and their organic grape vines (above).

Grape vines, ponds, and vegetation barriers on the family's certified agroecological property.

Dona Salete speaking about her family's experience transitioning from tobacco production to agroecology.

of that. And I am proud to walk on my farm today … an area that's clean and free of agrotoxins. That gives me pride.

Salete adds,

It makes us feel good about ourselves … what gives me the certainty to carry on is for the health of us, for my children, for my grandchildren, and for the people who buy our produce … it's wonderful to show that we are able to work without agrotoxins.

Dona Salete's and Seu Aluísio's experience with the negative effects of agrotoxins is unfortunately not uncommon. Yet, as recognition of the social and environmental costs of industrial agriculture grows, new social movements have emerged that experiment with alternatives and possibilities for new food systems in Brazil and around the world — ones that are less harmful and more aligned with social and environmental well-being.

CORPORATE POWER: PUTTING PROFIT OVER PEOPLE AND PLANET

So, it is safe to say that although modern technological advances and industrial logics have led to an enormous amount of "cheap" food, they have not successfully "fed the world" and come at a great expense to human and environmental health. The question to ask, then, is: "Why haven't we changed course if there are so many known problems associated with the industrial food system?" The key reason is that there are many powerful economic actors with a vested interest in maintaining the system as it is (such as agrifood corporations), because the industrial food system is highly profitable for them, despite the negative impacts borne by people and nature.[45] The market share captured by these large firms means that they wield enormous power (for example, through lobbying) "to set the terms of debate and thus to defend the status quo."[46]

The cluster of corporations who profit from the industrial food system are often referred to as key actors in the "corporate food regime."[47] These powerful multinational corporations (such as Bayer-Monsanto, ChemChina-Syngenta, Cargill, and Nestlé) exert influence over agrifood markets, set research funding priorities,[48] and shape national and international policies so that there are fewer protections for workers and the environment and also so that capital and goods can more easily flow across borders (known as trade liberalization). The result has been an increased emphasis on export-oriented production for sale on the global market. Neoliberal policies and increased global trade have therefore enabled the globalization of industrial agriculture — it is now the dominant form of agriculture practised in almost every corner of the world. This arrangement benefits the corporations, entrenches reliance on Green Revolution technologies, and directs profits to the wealthy nations, which host the corporations at the expense of farmers and food workers — especially in the Global South — who often struggle to make ends meet.[49]

Supporters of the corporate food regime argue that we cannot feed the world without industrial agriculture. However, the evidence shows that small-scale and more diverse farms are more productive and ecologically sustainable than large-scale and industrial farms,[50] especially in the long-term, given the tendency for industrial agriculture to undermine its own capacity to produce food. While Brazil is a prime example for showing the dangers associated with industrial food systems, particularly the need to get off the "pesticide treadmill," we can also look to Brazilian farmers (like Salete and Aluísio) for examples of how to transition toward a different food system that respects people and nature.

IN SEARCH OF "REAL UTOPIAS"

What has contributed to the emergence of such strong alternatives to industrial agriculture (like agroecology) in Brazil and other countries in the Global South? As mentioned, industrialization and globalization have not played out evenly across the world for a number of reasons. For example, some places are more integrated into global markets and supply chains; others less so. Some places have heterogeneous landscapes (think hilly or steep topography, varying soil types, inconsistent access to water) that do not lend themselves particularly well to standardization; others less so. Some places have policies or incentives that encourage farmers to adopt industrial management practices for commodity production for the global market; others less so. And some places have more active social movements and civil society organizations that resist industrialization and globalization.

These spaces — the ones that, for any of the above reasons or others, have fostered alternative kinds of food systems more firmly rooted in social justice and ecological principles — are *real utopias*.[51] Erik Olin Wright's concept of real utopias urges us to look to examples within the world as it currently exists to paint a picture of possible alternatives to problems caused by capitalism, including those caused by industrial agriculture. Alternative, place-based food systems can be considered "niches" that have cropped up in the cracks or margins — or what Wright calls "interstitial spaces" — of the dominant industrial food system. From this perspective, "utopia" — a term that conjures an association with impossibility — may not yet exist in its entirety, but examples of it exist in the real, on-the-ground initiatives being undertaken by individuals, communities, and social movements in these interstitial spaces. These alternative initiatives, while often small-scale, aim to counter some of the more harmful aspects of contemporary society, such as extreme inequality and the destruction of our life-support systems.

Throughout the rest of this book, we highlight an important cluster of real utopias that make up the agroecology movement in southern Brazil. The majority of these real utopias were identified through farmer networks that extend across the region, largely centred around the work of CEPAGRO and Centro Vianei, the community partners that helped make this book possible. As the political charter that emerged out of the 2018 meeting of the National Agroecology Alliance (Articulação Nacional de Agroecologia, ANA) in Brazil notes: "Youth present at the meeting made it clear that agroecology is a *real utopia*: based in their own experiences, which express coherence between agroecological discourse and practice, they pointed out pathways for rejuvenating agriculture and agrifood systems, respecting the diversity of ways of life."[52]

The success of agroecological real utopias at providing healthy and nutritious food, improving rural livelihoods, and enhancing ecological processes has led to agroecology[53] — once considered a fringe concept among the "world of ideas" about food systems — being increasingly discussed in policy spaces. Some world leaders are now describing agroecology as not only promising but also *necessary* if the world is going to successfully adapt to pressures from climate change and unsustainable resource consumption. For instance, the Food and Agriculture Organization (FAO) of the United Nations,[54] the High-Level Panel of Experts on Food Security and Nutrition (HLPE) of the UN Committee on World Food Security,[55] and other international scientific authorities such as the International Panel of Experts on Sustainable Food Systems (IPES-Food)[56] have in recent years argued that agroecology is necessary for a sustainable food future. The process of getting there involves a planned transition away from an industrial food system and toward an agroecological one.

It is clear that industrialization has come to shape and characterize the modern food system: the tractor reduced the amount of human labour required to tend fields; the assembly line method was incorporated into large-scale food manufacturing and processing plants; and technologies like pasteurization and refrigeration made it possible to store and transport large quantities of foods, like dairy, that otherwise would easily spoil. But the industrial, and now globalized, food system has contributed to multiple and overlapping social, health, economic, and environmental crises, especially as a result of Green Revolution technologies, neoliberal policies, and concentrated corporate control. The costs of these crises — or the negative externalities associated with the industrial food system — have been unfairly passed on to the public. Paradoxically, many of these same crises ultimately undermine the very conditions upon which the agrifood system depends, as is made clear by the case of CAFOs and the pesticide treadmill. Equally paradoxical is the fact that while we now produce more food than ever before, two billion people still do not have regular access to adequate food, while another two billion people experience malnutrition in the form of overweight or obesity. In short, the industrial food system does not appear to be feeding the world; rather, the corporations that wield enormous market power and control the food system have been accruing massive profits at the expense of people and the planet. However, farmers and workers on the front lines, like Salete and Aluísio, are (re)asserting their right to grow food in a way that respects ñature and provides them with dignified, healthy lives — putting agroecology into action.

Chapter 3

WHERE DOES AGROECOLOGICAL FOOD COME FROM?

Food produced by the industrial food system — the kind you'd find in most grocery stores — has been called "food from nowhere."[1] This means that the food products that we buy at the grocery store are made up of indistinguishable commodities and can be difficult to trace. For example, it is impossible to know exactly which farms grew the corn in your cornflakes; the corn in your cereal might as well have come from "nowhere." In contrast, agroecological food comes from "somewhere"[2] — you can frequently trace, say, the onion you bought back to a specific farm and farmer. For example, in the photo on the next page you can see that the onions on the market stand were grown by Juliano Cugnier.

Levels 2 and 3 of Gliessman's transition model correspond to farms that "substitute alternative practices for industrial/conventional inputs and practices" and/or "redesign the agroecosystem so that it functions on the basis of a new set of ecological processes."[3] In short, these are the places that are responsible for providing us with "food from somewhere." We highlight some of the real utopias exemplifying Levels 2 and 3, ranging from a relatively large grain farm that is experimenting with agroecological methods, to traditional populations keeping important cultural heritage practices alive, and farmer networks that are building collective capacity for food system change.

PARTICIPATORY GUARANTEE SYSTEMS

Before going any further, it is important to learn about Rede Ecovida (Ecolife Network), as many of the farmers and organizers featured in this book (though not all) are members of this network. Rede Ecovida is one of the world's first official participatory guarantee systems (PGS) and is a global reference point for participatory approaches to agroecological certification. Most consumers are already at least somewhat familiar with "organic" labels on food for sale. There are specific rules for how vendors can label their foods as organic and what the term organic means. In order to be able to use the organic label, farmers go through a process of organic certification, which guarantees that certain practices — those that are

Agroecological onions at a market in Florianópolis, advertising not only the produce but also who it was grown by — in this case, Juliano.

codified in the organic standards — are followed on the farm. In many places around the world, including Brazil, Canada, and the United States, most farmers go through the "third-party" auditing system in order to get certified as organic, where an external inspector visits the property to verify that the practices on the farm match what the farmer has described in their management plan (such as what kinds of foods are produced on the farm and which inputs are used). Once a farm has been certified, it can use the organic label on its products. In Brazil, the organic label indicates that the farm is acting in line with the organic standards set by the Brazilian government, which bans the use of certain types of agrichemicals (for instance, synthetic pesticides, fertilizers, and other types of soil amendments) and mandates certain animal welfare requirements.

As an alternative approach to the third-party certification system, Rede Ecovida created a unique, grassroots way of certifying farms based on peer-to-peer learning, relationship-building, and trust. In Rede Ecovida, members of the network — made up of farmers but also eaters, extension agents, and non-profit organizations — actively shape the standards for certification and are themselves responsible for certifying farms within the network as agroecological.

This participatory approach to certifying agroecological foods differs in a number of ways from the more typical third-party organic certification system. While the documentation in a management plan can be fairly onerous for both third-party and participatory certification, third-party certification requires less time overall because it relies on the

Members of a Rede Ecovida nucleo (the regional group, composed of many smaller and locally based groups) at their regional meeting in the neighbourhood of Ratones, Florianópolis.

findings of a hired inspector, who normally visits only once per year. However, third-party certification is usually significantly more expensive than participatory certification. Then again, the participatory system is much more time-intensive for the farmers. Members of the network meet regularly, and typically the meetings rotate among member farms so that the farmers get to visit the properties of their peers to learn about their growing methods.

A meeting of a Rede Ecovida nucleo. Here the farmers are discussing and scheduling dates to visit and verify the practices of other farmers in the network.

A meeting of a grupo *(group), the smallest collective unit within Rede Ecovida. Grupo meetings are held on a rotating basis at members' properties.*

They also frequently collaborate with one another to create processing centres or cooperatives, develop local organic markets or community-supported agriculture (CSA) programs, and aim to generally raise the profile of agroecology in Brazil. The high level of engagement required of the PGS participants makes it a more "social" pathway to certification. While organic farmers certified through third-party systems can reduce their certification to simply an economic transaction if they so choose, for Rede Ecovida, "certification is a pedagogical process where farmers, consultants, and eaters come together, and the quality of the certification is co-developed."[4]

Another thing that makes the PGS different from the third-party organic certification model is the range of practices that fall under the purview of certification. Many PGS assess farms according to agroecological principles, which go beyond technical farming practices by incorporating broader ecological concerns and considering social and political dynamics. For example, to be certified as agroecological with Rede Ecovida, a farmer is required to describe not only the specific management practices they use to enhance biodiversity, build soil, and protect water sources, but also the relationship to their workers and any training opportunities they provide to them. In addition, Rede Ecovida farmers are given a five-year period within which they are expected to have fully transitioned their property to agroecological

A typical grupo *meeting entails a tour of the host's property so that members can ask questions and share ideas and tips.*

management. This means that, after five years of transition, they are not permitted to have parallel production (separate fields on their property where they produce industrially grown foods in addition to the agroecological foods they grow). In contrast, organic farmers are able to produce industrial and agroecological foods in separate fields on their properties indefinitely, provided there is a buffer between them; there is no requirement to fully transition their property to organic management. In the words of Rede Ecovida farmer Daphne, in this sense, "the [Ecovida] network is more demanding than the law."

About 4,000 farm families make up Rede Ecovida. The network is spread across Brazil's three southernmost states — Rio Grande do Sul, Santa Catarina, and Paraná — and has been expanding into the state of São Paulo. The model has many benefits: it is low-cost (since farmers do not have to pay for third-party inspectors), transparent, inclusive of multiple food stakeholders, brings participants onto farms, and facilitates network-building and peer-to-peer learning.

On the other hand, Rede Ecovida members do describe the process as time-consuming, which can be a barrier for growers who are already committed to the time- and labour-intensive management activities (for example, manual weeding) that come along with not using industrial practices. By certifying through Rede Ecovida, growers still receive state-recognized organic certification through Brazil's Ministry of Agriculture, Livestock, and Supply (Ministério da Agricultura, Pecuária e Abastecimento, MAPA), which accepts either participatory certification or third-party certification. As a result, farmers involved in the PGS can benefit from organic price premiums and preferential access to public procurement programs, such as the National School Feeding Program (Programa Nacional de Alimentação Escolar, PNAE), just like those who certify through third parties. In the following story, we further describe PNAE and how it has created a new market for agroecological and organic farmers in Brazil.

MONICA AND DEOGENIO: PUBLIC POLICIES FOR AGROECOLOGY

Seu Deogenio and Dona Monica, two farmers in their sixties, live on a six hectare property in the western region of Santa Catarina. Most of their income comes from the farm, but they both also receive retiree pensions — although the rural pension program, which is a very important source of income for many elderly rural workers, has been significantly and negatively modified by the administration of the current president, Jair Bolsonaro.[5] They inherited the farm from Deogenio's parents, who had a dairy operation and used most of the land for grazing.

They wanted to start farming organically when they took over the farm about fifteen years ago, but it was challenging and "*não dava*" ("it wasn't working"). Seven or eight years after that, they sold all their cows and tried again, and this time persevered: "Then we got rid of that nightmare. Because we didn't want to be using agrichemicals." Nevertheless, the quality of the land had degraded quite a bit from overgrazing, so once they began transitioning the property toward agroecological management the second time it still "took four, five years for the land to recover." This illustrates how the process of transitioning from industrial toward agroecological methods is often nonlinear. There are many ups and downs, especially in the first few years as the agroecosystem

Dona Monica holding a perfectly ripe amora *(blackberry).*

Seu Deogenio connects with one of their heifers.

finds a new equilibrium and restabilizes after recovering from industrial management. Because of the challenges that occur during the transition, especially within the first couple of years, many farmers begin to adopt agroecological practices but then revert to industrial practices for any number of reasons — for example, because the learning curve is steep, or because of insufficient labour, or because the lower yields or prices during the transition period are not economically viable. But in due time they might try to integrate some agroecological practices again — perhaps because demand for organic produce increases, or policy incentives are introduced, or the health costs of agrichemical use become too severe. Overall, transitioning from industrial to agroecological management takes a lot of initiative, patience, and perseverance (and often, support — either from family or neighbours, cooperatives, or government).

While they have been farming agroecologically for the past fifteen years or so, Monica and Deogenio were in the middle of the process of actually becoming certified as an agroecological farm through Rede Ecovida when we met them. They now have a few cows for their own dairy consumption, which they graze in rotation, and practice agroforestry — a technique that integrates crops and/or animals with trees and shrubs in order to grow food in a way that mimics a forest ecosystem. In addition, they have very diversified vegetable fields; after starting to list the various crops they were growing, they gave up and said, "You can try to count, but you'll lose count. But it's a lot."

The only crops that they sell are banana and papaya, which they bring to their local cooperative; the rest of what they grow they keep for themselves and their family. The cooperative then distributes their fruit to local schools as part of the National School Feeding Program. While the PNAE has existed since the 1950s, the Luiz Inácio Lula da Silva ("Lula") administration revamped the program in 2009 and committed to sourcing at least 30 percent of school food from local family farmers. This program, called a public procurement program since it directs public institutions to procure goods in line with specific policy objectives, created a mediated market for family farmers by connecting them directly to the institutional purchasing needs and demands of local schools.[6] The market is "mediated" in that the state intervenes and dictates some of the terms of the purchasing protocol, which in this case includes a mandate to purchase from local family farmers. The Lula administration also modified the PNAE to further incentivize organic and agroecological farming methods: farmers using these methods receive a price premium for their products as well as preferential access to PNAE contracts.[7]

While the success of public procurement programs has been imperfect due to limited implementation (failing to reach many marginalized communities, for instance), these kinds of policy innovations play an important role in encouraging farmers to transition away from industrial agricultural methods and toward diversified, agroecological systems.[8]

Seu Deogenio and Dona Monica's more established agroforestry plot (toward the back) and the newly planted plot in the foreground.

Eventually, Dona Monica and Seu Deogenio will sell these bananas to a local school through the PNAE.

Unfortunately, many of the programs that were scaled up in the early to mid-2000s to support small-scale family farms and organic or agroecological production have since been rolled back due to political instability and the re-entrenchment of neoliberal policies in Brazil that largely prioritize export-oriented industrial agriculture. This demonstrates how, depending on the kind of intervention, government policies and programs can play either an enabling or inhibiting role in supporting agroecological transitions.

HELITON: FROM TOBACCO MONOCULTURES TO DIVERSIFIED FARMING

Another government program that has helped many rural farmers in Brazil is the Banco da Terra (Land Bank) program. Heliton's family acquired 17 hectares of property in 2000 through Banco da Terra, which provides financing options for individuals or collectives to purchase agricultural land, build or finance basic necessities (like housing, roads, and water systems), and access technical training. The program is unique in a number of ways, including the fact that it's only available to landless rural workers or small-scale farmers who have a history in rural areas and intend to stay in the countryside to farm.

When Heliton's family purchased the land from the Land Bank it was already being used for *fumicultura* (tobacco production). Although they had not intended to produce tobacco, they started to do so since the infrastructure on the property was set up for it. As Heliton describes,

> When we came here, since everything was already in place for tobacco production, we had to work with tobacco because that is what we had. But my father never wanted to, the idea was never to work with tobacco. But it wasn't until my father became poisoned from agrichemicals that he decided to radically change things.

Like Seu Aluísio, Heliton's father became *intoxicado* (sick) from the agrichemicals used during tobacco production and from handling the tobacco directly. The poisoning of Heliton's father was a turning point. He explains, "Overnight we stopped with everything and we started to produce using organic methods, in 2001." Following this, Heliton's father became a renowned agroecology advocate and social movement organizer in the central region of Santa Catarina. However, Heliton has taken over the management of the farm recently because his father's health has significantly declined, due in no small part to the agrotoxins to which he had long been exposed from tobacco production.

Today, Heliton and his family own 13.5 hectares of land — seven of which are in crops,

Heliton (left) and his partner as they took a break to speak with us in the fields.

The old tobacco processing and drying barn on Heliton's property, now in a state of disrepair as they have abandoned tobacco production and transitioned to a diversified system.

three of which in pasture, and with the rest preserved as forest, as per the legal requirements of Brazil's forest code, which stipulates that 20 percent of a rural property should be forested. Heliton, with two other family members and two hired workers, is farming entirely according to agroecological principles. At the moment, this means that much of the labour on their property is manual labour, because most agricultural research and funding has gone toward providing technological solutions more appropriate to large-scale, industrialized, and simplified farms. Because of the lack of scale-appropriate and accessible technologies that are suited to diversified, rather than monocultural, cropping systems, combined with the often arduous nature of manual farm work and the trend of rural-to-urban migration (especially of young people), labour typically emerges as a major cost or constraint for agroecological and organic farms.

Heliton's fields are mostly organized in rows of diverse crops, but one of the fields is still covered with crop stubble, into which workers directly seed the next crop — a technique known locally as *plantio direto*. Cutting through the fields are flower strips populated with a diversity of native plants. These flower strips provide a good example of *multifunctionality*, a key concept in the design of agroecosystems. Multifunctionality refers to the fact that

A hired worker hoeing in Heliton's fields.

agroecosystems and their components serve multiple purposes beyond food production. In this case, the flower strips provide multiple functions in that they are aesthetically pleasing, they increase on-farm biodiversity, attract beneficial insects like bees and other pollinators, and the flowers could be harvested and sold. They also serve as part of a larger integrated pest management (IPM) strategy that reduces pests (such as aphids) by harbouring their natural enemies (like ladybugs). Surrounding the fields is a vegetation barrier of native trees that is being used to prevent any agrichemicals sprayed by the conventional neighbours from drifting over to Heliton's farm. This practice — having a vegetation barrier that separates conventional farms and fields from organic or agroecologically managed fields — is a requirement for receiving agroecological certification through Rede Ecovida.

Today, Heliton and his family sell their produce locally and in Florianópolis, as well as to the municipal government through the PNAE. In contrast to producing commercial tobacco for export markets, they are now bolstering regional food security while protecting the health of their family, workers, and the local environment.

Two workers on Heliton's farm transplanting young plants directly into the prior crop's stubble.

A flower strip that attracts bees and other helpful insects runs through the middle of Heliton's field, while native trees form a barrier to prevent chemical drift from neighbours using conventional methods.

PABLO: EXPERIMENTATION WITH AGROECOLOGICAL FARMING

Like Heliton, Pablo is another young farmer. He works with one hired worker and his father, who has been farming conventional grains on the 300 hectares they own spread across two sites. Because Pablo's farm is relatively large for the region and the fields have been in grain production, they have been able to benefit from some technologies (a tractor and combine) to support them in planting and harvesting.

Pablo went to study traditional agronomy at a university in Santa Catarina, with the plan of returning to the farm. Yet, not long after graduating, he was introduced to the science and practice of agroecology through a friend of a friend. Pablo has since convinced his father that they should transition to agroecological farming methods:

> Pablo: Within these 300 hectares, we are well in transition. We basically produce grain. In winter we have been producing wheat, white oats, black oats, peas, forage, some vetch, barley, rye — what we're producing here depends on the year … and in the summer it's basically soy and corn.

> Evan: Are you organic here in this area?

Pablo and a hired worker unjamming their combine on one of their grain fields.

Pablo drives a combine over one of their large grain fields, into which they will directly seed the next crop.

Pablo: No, this area is conventional. But despite being conventional, there are several transition factors that we address. We no longer apply synthetic fungicides ... that ends up reducing our production cost a lot. Our system is not [certified] organic in these 270 hectares but we bring a lot of the organic practices into the system.

So, a first step for many farmers is to experiment with agroecology by adopting specific practices on a small subset of their farm or to become more efficient by substituting an agro-ecological practice for an industrial one across their farm — for example, replacing tillage practices that use a tractor to turn the soil with no-till or direct seeding. In Santa Catarina, there has been a sustained effort on the part of the state government's extension agency, the Company of Agricultural Research and Rural Extension of Santa Catarina (Empresa de Pesquisa Agropecuária e Extensão Rural de Santa Catarina, EPAGRI), to reach out to and work with farmers to adopt direct seeding. This method protects valuable topsoil from erosion, builds soil fertility through organic matter, and can help reduce weeds. However, implementing this practice at a larger scale often requires expensive, proprietary, fossil-fuel dependent machinery, and no-till systems can still require agrichemicals to manage pests.

While Pablo's father is supportive of his ideas and methods, Pablo is very much the pro-tagonist of the transition on their property:

[My father] supports me a lot in all the actions I'm taking. But the focus on agro-ecology research is mine ... He does end up getting involved because there is no way not to get involved, right? At times he tells me we have to clean up the fields because they are very messy and he says they will not produce, but I believe that within four or five years it will be super beautiful and my father will say that I was right and that I was not going crazy.

Pablo's reflections here touch upon what can often go unrecognized as a barrier in the transition toward organic or agroecological methods: stigma. A number of farmers we spoke with mentioned that they occasionally were the targets of peer pressure or even mockery by their relatives, neighbours, or friends who farm with conventional methods and think that agroecologically managed fields appear disorderly relative to the manicured monocultures of industrial agriculture. For this reason, many participants in the agroecology movement describe the difficulty in changing other farmers' mindsets or philosophies as one of the biggest factors inhibiting more people from adopting agroecology. It is similarly difficult to change consumer expectations; when Pablo was asked about the potential for agroecology to take off, he said that he thinks changes are happening, but that it will take a long time:

First you have to change the minds of the people, a lot. Because organic is still not a philosophy for most of the population, and if the consumer does not ask for organic, the market doesn't want to offer it. And if you do a survey of how many people you know [in Brazil] who consume organic foods? It's very few, right. So, I think it will to some extent be a bit on the consumers' end to help activate the demand for organic

Pablo is experimenting with agroforestry, grapes, and corn grown using two different methods.

production. Here in town my father and I are aliens doing this more organic grain production. People don't even know what it is, they don't know where to sell it — there's still a long way to go.

Pablo in an organic soy field.

For Pablo's part, he's convinced that agroecology is the future, and has dedicated himself to learning more about and experimenting with agroecological methods. For instance, on one part of the property he is building a cob house (a natural building method) to host farmer gatherings and has planted an area following principles from permaculture and syntropic agroforestry (a no-input system which aims to mimic processes of ecological succession in forests by cultivating diverse plant communities). In this part of the farm, Pablo is growing grapes, native cherries, apples, figs, plums, oranges, bergamot, lemons, pecans, and more. In the organic grain fields nearby, he's experimenting with numerous cover crop mixtures to see which mix provides the optimal conditions for his corn and soy.

In contrast to standardized industrial management, Pablo's willingness to test new growing methods, observe the results, and change his management practices accordingly speaks to the importance of experimentation, ongoing learning, and adaptive management in agroecological farming.

CLEBER: THE CHALLENGES OF ORGANIC LIVESTOCK

When we met Cleber, he was raising twenty-five cattle (eighteen of which were dairy cows) in the western part of Santa Catarina, a region that has a fairly strong livestock sector. He comes from a family farming background, and at that time he and his family owned 17 hectares of land. Around eleven of these hectares were already certified as organic pasture, managed as a rotational grazing system of almost ninety *piquetes* (paddocks). Cleber was also in the process of transitioning his annual grain fields to organic management so that he could supplement the diet of his herd with organic feed in addition to grass. Of the remaining area of his property, a few hectares were in native forest or reforested, again in line with Brazil's forest code.

Despite raising the dairy herd organically, Cleber and his family were selling the milk as conventional, and thus were not receiving an organic price premium. There were a number of reasons for this. One is that certified organic milk needs to be collected, processed, and distributed entirely separately from conventional milk, to ensure that the two don't mix. This essentially means that organic milk requires a totally separate infrastructure than conventional milk, with the onus often placed on organic farmers to create or find those facilities — a costly investment. Another reason is that, being in the far western part of the state, it's too expensive for Cleber to transport his milk to Florianópolis, the coastal capital of Santa Catarina and the closest major domestic market where consumers might be willing or able to pay the higher price for organic milk. Around where he lives, this isn't the case. As Cleber explains,

> Being an extremely agricultural region in the interior of the state, there is not such a noticeable difference in price between organic and conventional production for several reasons, including cultural and financial reasons. Generally speaking, if we look for recent values, the value [of organic milk] is triple [that of conventional milk]. We don't have that here.

So, despite following all of the protocols for producing organic milk, Cleber has not been

A wooden post marking a piquete, *with the rolling hills of São Miguel do Oeste, Santa Catarina, in the background.*

Cleber flooded a small area on his property to provide some water access. Some of his cattle are grazing in a piquete *in the background.*

able to benefit by receiving a higher price. To try to get around this problem, Cleber was in the process of organizing with a few other local organic dairy producers in order to jumpstart an organic milk cooperative where they could aggregate their production and make it worth the cost and effort of transporting their milk to Florianópolis. He said,

> We still face difficulties. But [those problems] could end through scale. If we had more producers, we could add more value by having more production and being able to produce more consistently through the seasons. That is to say, the production wouldn't be so up and down. So, this is the difficulty, the fall in value of production and the lack of monetary added value. Also, because there is a transition period for organic certification of eighteen months. So, there are eighteen months of suffering [as you wait to be able to sell at the higher price].

Because of Cleber's interests in politics and the need to supplement his income and support his retired mother and uncle, he had also sought out a position as a municipal councillor. When we last touched base, Cleber noted that the demands of his off-farm work for the municipality combined with the responsibility of managing his family's farm almost

A rogue bull needed to be walked back to pasture.

single-handedly led to the decision to sell almost all of their cows. While they still manage most of the property organically, they are now leasing 6 hectares of land to their neighbour. Now, most of Cleber's effort is spent supporting the local group of organic producers and the fledgling dairy cooperative in the hopes that collectivizing their efforts can lead to new market opportunities and a more sustainable local dairy sector. However, the pressure that small- to medium-scale agroecological dairy farms are under to compete with larger-scale, more capitalized, and industrialized milk producers — all while following the even more stringent organic standards — is a major obstacle in the transition to agroecological food systems.

IRIMAR: RAISING ORGANIC POULTRY AT SCALE

Irimar is another organic animal farmer. He inherited his 3.6 hectare property in 2017, and, while it had not been farmed conventionally in the recent past, it was nonetheless in a bit of disarray when he took over. In Irimar's words:

Here the land is broken. Everything is on a slope. It is a land that was worth nothing to farmers. That's why we made a point of doing it here, to prove that it is possible for a small-scale farmer to survive in a small area. This is one of our purposes … My brothers-in-law were using it but weren't mowing it, and they also weren't using herbicides on anything … the land was like that for twelve years.

Despite the challenges, Irimar and his family were immediately able to certify the property as organic since there had not been a recent history of non-permitted agrichemical use. In contrast, if agrichemicals are used in the recent past, the process of certification takes more time — usually a couple of years of producing without prohibited substances before a farm is eligible for certification. But since this wasn't the case for Irimar's family, they began raising laying hens and were certified to produce organic eggs. They now have around 1,000 hens — a sizable organic egg operation.

While they initially had their production certified through Ecocert, a third-party certification body, they had begun attending Rede Ecovida meetings and intended to shift to the participatory certification model:

Irimar: We were certified from the beginning through Ecocert. We want to move to Ecovida, though. We got certified at the end of 2017 … but the idea is to go to Ecovida now; we are already going to the meetings and everything. We believe that participatory certification is the most authentic. The auditor [from Ecocert] comes

A view of Irimar's layer barns, recently constructed for his hens.

here once a year and we pay 4,000 reais [Can$1500] and it's a strange business, in my opinion.

Dana: It's 4,000 reais to certify with Ecocert?

Irimar: Yes — 4000 and a bit. And that's in partnership with AGRECO[9] [a local farmers' association for organic farmers], which sells the feed to me. If [I did it independently], it would be more expensive.

In addition to the cost of certification, Irimar spends a lot of money on organic feed for the chickens, which is a criterion for certification. While Irimar supplements his hens' diet with vegetable scraps from their garden, he mostly relies on organic corn that he purchases through AGRECO. This is, by far, his most significant cost. He reported that the organic feed he buys costs 120 percent more than non-organic (conventional) feed, which is a big barrier for farmers who would like to raise livestock and poultry organically.

Irimar in one of his layer barns.

Another specific challenge faced by organic poultry and livestock farmers relates to developing methods for dealing with illness and disease. The organic standards place limitations on what kinds of synthetic drugs or remedies farmers can use to treat sick animals. As a result, organic and agroecological farmers heavily invest in preventative measures that improve animal welfare and minimize the risk of disease and transmission. This includes but is not limited to providing adequate space for natural animal movement and behaviours, lowering stock density, and allowing access to the outdoors.

Irimar has a number of strategies in place to ensure the health and well-being of his hens. First, as per the organic standards, his hens have a lot of space to move around — about 4.5 to 5 metres per hen. The animal welfare benefits of this are immediately obvious, especially when compared to the inhumane treatment of chickens in CAFOs, where hens spend their lives densely packed into cages. They also have continuous access to the outdoors, where they rotate through various *piquetes* to avoid overgrazing and over-fertilizing.

Second, Irimar creates various homeopathic remedies to try to prevent illness. He explains:

Irimar and his family showing their packaged organic eggs, ready for market.

We carry out a weekly rotation. One week we beat garlic in the blender and strain in the morning and put a little in the water tank. This helps the chickens not have the flu. There is also lemon with honey. We put 700 ml of lemon and 700 ml of honey, also in the water tank … There is also mint tea that we make for worms. And there's banana leaf tea … We used to not do this treatment. Then they got a disease, a year ago now. So we do this treatment every two days. Even when they were very sick, we would put it in their mouths … And this year there was no disease. When they moult they have lower immunity, so the disease could have returned, but so far it has not … This kind of knowledge [about homeopathy] is more word-of-mouth. When the hens got sick here, the guidance that extension services gave me was only about antibiotics. There is no guidance on homeopathy from the government.

Because such little public and private funding and research has gone into understanding and supporting the needs of organic livestock and poultry producers, in many ways, Irimar has to rely on his own experiences and the experiences of fellow agroecological farmers to get a sense for what works for treating animals and stopping the spread of diseases. If one of Irimar's hens gets sick, Irimar places her in a little quarantine chamber until her health improves, in order to maintain the health of the other hens. These kinds of measures are increasingly important as intensive, industrial animal agriculture — where animal populations are becoming increasingly genetically uniform and are housed in CAFOs — can contribute to the emergence of novel pathogens,[10] as has been the case with recent epidemics of swine and avian influenzas. As these epidemics and the COVID-19 pandemic have shown, novel

Hens eating organic grain at a feeder.

pathogens can be extremely costly in terms of human and non-human lives, as well as in terms of economic losses.

The lack of government and extension support, the preventative management of disease, and the cost of inputs like organic animal feed make the challenges facing agroecological and organic livestock and poultry farmers substantial. But the farmer-to-farmer learning that occurs across social networks and through experimentation, as well as the ability to purchase bulk inputs thanks to supportive agricultural cooperatives, has made a big difference for Irimar.

In addition to traditional family farms like those we've discussed so far, there are also a number of other rural populations and collectives that are practising agroecology in southern Brazil. In the following stories, we introduce *extrativistas* (people using traditional and sustainable harvesting practices) and two groups that have implemented collective forms of agriculture.

The hens have constant access to outdoor pasture.

Sick hens are temporarily isolated from the rest of the flock in order to eliminate the risk of disease transmission.

EXTRATIVISMO: SUSTAINABLE HARVESTING OF *PINHÃO* (BRAZILIAN PINE NUT)

By Natal João Magnanti, PhD, Project Coordinator, Vianei Popular Education Centre

The Atlantic Forest biome, which includes much of southern and southeastern Brazil, is a global biodiversity hotspot. The mixed ombrophilous forest (FOM) is a specific ecosystem within this biome that is severely under threat from deforestation, particularly due to timber harvesting.[11] The *Araucaria* (Brazilian pine), which produces the *pinhão* (pine nut), is an important and endangered species in the FOM.[12] The gravity of this situation demands measures that will enable the conservation of this ecosystem.

Extrativismo (sustainable harvesting) has been a part of people's strategy for food security since time immemorial. With the recent recognition of biodiversity as an economic, environmental, and cultural asset, sustainable harvesting is attracting increased attention as a means to combine biodiversity conservation with culturally relevant, income-generating livelihoods.[13] Sustainable extraction is understood as the collection of species of interest by local populations, in which extraction rates do not exceed the species' production capacity and do not harm the stability of the ecosystem. In this way, sustainable extraction plays a role in agroecological transitions.

The extraction of non-timber forest products (NTFP) has a social, cultural, and gastronomic character and is an economic activity practised by thousands of families. In fact, one of the ways to conserve ecologically important species is through the sustainable extraction

Araucaria trees dot the landscape throughout Santa Catarina. It is illegal to cut these trees down due to their endangered and protected status.

Araucaria trees (right foreground) viewed from above in the Planalto Serrano Catarinense, Santa Catarina.

of NTFP, like Brazilian pine nuts. In the Planalto Serrano Catarinense (PSC) region,[14] family farmers are the main group partaking in the extraction of pine nuts,[15] making them an important social actor for the conservation of native biodiversity. Traditional communities — a specific designation in Brazil used for groups with a relationship to territory and sustainable development, including Indigenous Peoples, Afro-Brazilian communities, river dwellers, family farmers, and *extratavistas* — can make lasting use of the wealth that can be sustainably extracted from the forest.[16]

Pinhão is an NTFP that, over the last few decades, has been increasing in social and economic importance as farm families use it for consumption but also for commercialization.[17] In other words, sustainable harvesting can assist in the conservation of the species as well as generate income for a significant portion of family farmers.[18]

The PSC includes the ten main *pinhão*-producing municipalities in Santa Catarina, contributing 75 percent of all production in the region. In 2017, municipalities in the territory sold 2,751 tonnes of pine nuts, generating revenue of 5.14 million reais (Can$1.95 million), sold at an average price of 2.17 reais/kilogram (Can$0.82).[19] Centro Vianei, an agroecological hub in the PSC, has been assisting family farmers and groups in the agroecological transition with a focus on sustainable NTFP extraction, especially with *Araucaria*.

Some people, like Seu Mario, practising extrativismo *do so on public lands. Here, Seu Mario is scaling an* Araucaria *tree to harvest* pinhão, *a traditional activity for many local communities in central Santa Catarina.*

Upon reaching the top, Seu Mario searches for pinhão seed pods (shown here) …

… and then uses a long, wooden pole to push the seed pods off the tree, where they fall to the ground far below.

A pinhão seed pod on the ground.

Individual pine nuts.

One traditional way to eat pinhão *is in the field, right after harvest. A bonfire is built using dried, dead* Araucaria *branches that have fallen to the ground. Then, the pine nuts are added.*

The bonfire is extinguished…

… and once the fire is put out, we're left with deliciously toasted and protein-rich pine nuts, ready to eat.

Others practising extrativismo, *like Seu Vilmar, harvest* pinhão *on their own properties and/or pay a small fee to access the properties of other people in the area.*

Seu Vilmar breaking up some seed pods …

…which he typically runs through a clever device he made that shakes the seed pods apart much more quickly than he could by hand alone.

Seu Mario takes a well-deserved break from his strenuous climb and skillful harvesting for a photo op in the treetops.

AGRARIAN MOVEMENTS: DEMOCRATIZING LAND ACCESS THROUGH COLLECTIVE STRUGGLE

While *extrativismo* often occurs on public land or through negotiated access to private lands, some of Brazil's social movements take a more radical approach to land access. An example is the Landless Rural Workers Movement (MST) of Brazil, one of the largest and best-known agrarian social movements in the world. It is a founding member of the international organization La Vía Campesina (LVC) and is a touchstone in the rich history of Brazilian social movements (along with other groups like the Movement of People Affected by Dams, MAB).

The MST is a highly organized movement that fights for access to land and land reform (or "agrarian reform"). Their tactics are highly subversive in that their main strategy is to occupy underutilized private lands. In much of the Brazilian popular media, the MST is criminalized — deemed "invaders" and "vagabonds" for what is positioned as collective property theft. This is a widespread sentiment in Brazil, despite the fact that the country has one of the highest rates of land inequality in the world: 73 percent of agricultural land is owned by only 10 percent of the landowners.[20] So when the MST organizes, they are fighting for a more equitable Brazil.

Brazil's colonial past is rife with the violent appropriation of large tracts of land. This history is one of rich aristocratic families who held giant estates (*latifundias*) of fertile agricultural land, while the agrarian working classes struggled to access land and were pushed into smaller production units in more marginal areas. A result of this historical struggle has been the emergence of collective organizations like the MST, who assert their "agrarian

An MST protest in Florianópolis.

citizenship" rights to produce food.[21] In recognizing these rights, Article 186 of the 1988 Brazilian constitution declares that land must be put to a "productive" use and should fulfil a "social function." It gave Brazilian citizens the constitutionally guaranteed right to use "unproductive" land if it is deemed to not be fulfilling its "social function" according to the following criteria: "Rational and adequate use (based on legislated norms of economic productivity); adequate use of available natural resources and preservation of the environment; compliance with labour regulations; and land-use that favours the well-being of the owners and labourers."[22]

This clause provides social movements like the MST with a legal basis to challenge underutilized large rural estates in Brazil by arguing that they are not meeting the criteria for fulfilling the social function. If it is proven that arable, privately owned lands are not fulfilling the social function, they can be expropriated by the state and redistributed to landless farmers, and possibly formally transferred to them through the National Institute for Colonization and Agrarian Reform (Instituto Nacional de Colonização e Reforma Agrária, INCRA). To this end, agrarian reform movements have often used the strategy of physically occupying such estates in order to draw attention to the issue and pressure the state to redistribute the land. As a result of their ongoing advocacy and tactics, the MST

The MST logo is painted on this settlement's schoolhouse in central Santa Catarina.

has been successful at getting land redistributed to peasant and formerly landless workers across Brazil. As Juliana Adriano — the Santa Catarina Education Coordinator of the MST — explains, in Santa Catarina alone,

> the MST now has about 6,000 families living in 140 settlements that occupy more than 70,000 hectares of land. In this space there are twenty-six schools, eight cooperatives, community radio stations, health centres and a lot of healthy food production.[23]

As a large and radical social movement, the MST depends on maintaining a set of norms and a system for socializing new members. To this end, and as Juliana mentioned, the MST runs its own schools and has developed its own critical pedagogical strategy, highly influenced by Brazilian educator and philosopher Paulo Freire.[24] The schools are usually constructed on settlements (that is, lands where landless workers and families have been "settled" by the state) and are places where members learn and enact principles of participatory democracy and agroecology, alongside other curricula.

The MST has long promoted ecological farm management alongside its sociopolitical agenda. It specifically promotes the use of agroecological practices, both in its schools and in the wider movement. Students graduate with an education that supplements the national

curriculum with farm management and training in agroecological management, preparing
them to be future farmers, extension agents,
movement leaders and activists, or even
policymakers.

There are other activist groups in Brazil,
similar to the MST, fighting against landless-
ness and for agrarian reform by asserting the
social function of land. One such example
is the collective at Assentamento Comuna
Amarildo de Souza. In 2013, sixty families
occupied an area of 600 hectares on Santa
Catarina Island, which hosts part of the capital city of Florianópolis — some of the most
valuable land in all of Brazil. A great struggle
happened on many fronts, including through
various protests and marches. Eventually the
group succeeded at securing land for them-

*This sweater worn by many of the students
at the school translates to "Agroecology
technician."*

selves but were relocated (twice) before finally being settled in 2015 on land about an
hour's drive outside of Florianópolis. Six families now live in the settlement and practice
collective agriculture according to agroecological principles.

These types of land occupation struggles are not uncommon in Brazil. But what makes
this case so interesting is its proximity to a densely populated urban centre. Throughout their
struggle for land, they have fought with government organizations ranging from the INCRA
to the power utility company (which denied their access to power for over a year once they
were settled). This, yet again, highlights how contentious competing land interests are — and
how the most valuable agricultural land often gets consolidated in the hands of only a subset
of elite landowners or lost to urban development pressures.

On the whole, in contrast to industrially produced food, agroecological food comes
"from somewhere." Certification schemes like the PGS play a role in communicating the
origins of, and methods used to grow, organic foods while also creating and strengthening
farmer networks. Public programs, policies, and agencies (like the Land Bank program,
PNAE, and INCRA) can play an important role in incentivizing or supporting farmers in the
transition to agroecology. For Irimar, Pablo, and Monica and Deogenio, the willingness to
experiment with different practices, to persevere despite social stigma, and to overcome
technical setbacks has been crucial to their transition processes. From Irimar's and Cleber's
experiences we also learned about the specific challenges for agroecological animal agriculture, including the high cost of organic inputs like feed, the difficulty in obtaining a feasible

Aerial view of one of the production areas in an agrarian reform settlement, Comuna Amarildo, which is mostly collectively farmed.

Val and his partner, who are members of Comuna Amarildo, harvesting produce at Comuna Amarildo.

scale of production and in dealing with infrastructure regulations, and the lack of formal research on how to treat diseases using organic-approved methods. *Extrativistas* like Mario and Vilmar, who use and pass down traditional practices for sustainably harvesting NTFP (in this case, pine nuts), also play a valuable role in maintaining biocultural heritage and diversity. Lastly, we shared stories about social movements' struggles to access land and democratize rural areas — one of the most contentious and longstanding issues shaping agrifood systems in Brazil.

Chapter 4

CREATING AND DEEPENING GROWER–EATER RELATIONS

L evel 4, a deeper level of transition, entails fostering new and more profound connections between urban–rural places and people. This speaks to how agroecological transitions involve more than just changing how we produce food; they need to connect rural and urban places to bring about a transformation of the industrial food system.

As the world has urbanized and industrialized, food from the countryside has been exported to major metropolises. This has left rural soils depleted, as the nutrients that were exported in the form of food to cities often ended up in landfills rather than being properly reincorporated back into the soils from which they were drawn. This process is often referred to as the *metabolic rift*.[1] Alongside the nutrients lost to the metabolic rift, a *knowledge rift* has developed as well, as rural workers have increasingly moved to cities in search of jobs.[2] Over time, this rural-to-urban migration (or what has been called the rural exodus) has disrupted and eroded the transmission of agricultural knowledge across generations, leaving urban people to often feel divorced from a connection to the land, food, and rural issues such as farmer and farm-worker welfare.

A stronger connection between growers and eaters is crucial for developing more environmentally sound and socially just food systems. Such relations can follow a number of pathways, including the creation of new market channels for agroecological food to come into the city; the development of spaces for urban people to engage with and learn about various aspects of the food system; and new opportunities for urban people to travel to, learn about, and support agroecological farmers in the countryside.

MERCADO SÃO JORGE: PRIVILEGED AGROECOLOGICAL CONSUMPTION

Down the street from CEPAGRO's headquarters is a large indoor market called Mercado São Jorge, known as one of the city's best places to procure agroecological foods. You can usually hear live music throughout the day, echoing over the intermingling customers as they stroll from shop to shop. There are several restaurants and bars in the market, as well as health product vendors and those selling artisanal jewellery and pottery. The place smells of freshly brewed coffee and local beer, and you can hear cutlery clinking as families out for lunch enjoy a delicious, albeit expensive, meal together. This is not a place where the majority of the city population shops. This is a space of social privilege — and this is a problem for agroecological food systems everywhere, not just in Brazil.

Those with the ability to purchase food here generally do so for one of two reasons. The first camp purchases organic foods for more personal reasons. Shoppers in this category are not necessarily aiming to support a transition to a different kind of food system. Rather, they are concerned about the potentially harmful health effects of eating food produced using agrichemicals, and so choose agroecological produce for themselves and their families because they are perceived to be safer, more nutritious, or tastier. These are the "foodies" among the eaters of agroecological foods.

A second category of people could be called "ethical consumers." These people purchase agroecological foods for more than just personal reasons — they value and want to encourage more environmentally friendly agricultural practices, or support small-scale family farmers, or ensure that farm workers are not exposed to harmful agrichemicals. Some scholars have called this a mode of "food citizenship," or responsible consumption,[3] which captures the efforts of those who "vote with their forks" (or, perhaps more accurately, with their wallets). This approach to food-systems change follows the logic of basic economic principles of supply and demand — if consumer demand for organic and agroecological food grows, then farmers will respond by increasing the supply. More agroecological food as a proportion of the total food produced means less "food from nowhere" will be produced, lowering the overall impact of the industrial food system.[4] This is one theory of change for how an eater-led agroecological transition could happen.

Of course, people do not necessarily fall into only one of these categories — this is a crude breakdown of motivations, and these categories should not be thought of as mutually exclusive. Consumers could both enjoy the potential health benefits of agroecological foods and also want to support local farmers and to support a transition toward more sustainable farming methods. However, regardless of the exact nature of the motivation to purchase agroecological foods, the underlying limitation with this approach to food-systems change is that it depends on the ability to purchase foods at a premium rate, at least in the interim, as agroecological systems transition away from industrial methods. Organic and agroecological foods are often more expensive and challenging to produce, transport, and store (since they often do not have chemical agents or preservatives protecting them from decomposition). Plus, there are costs associated with labour inputs and certification (although some forms of certification are more affordable than others). And so, the prices of organic and agroecological foods are often higher to reflect this. In other words, rather than externalize the social and environmental costs of production, the full costs of production are internalized,

Beautiful, but pricey, agroecologically grown peppers in Mercado Sao Jorge. The peppers were roughly triple the price of non-organic ones at the local supermarkets.

which typically makes these foods more expensive than their industrial counterparts. And all too frequently, grocery stores and restaurants that offer organic and agroecological foods, like Mercado São Jorge, specifically cater to those with relative privilege and the disposable income to consume these pricier products.

One way that agroecology movements try to disrupt the limitations of consumption-driven change is by referring to the people who consume agroecological foods as "eaters" rather than consumers. The term "consumer" reduces an individual to *homo economicus* within a commodified capitalist system. It also erases the political agency that people have (albeit constrained) to make not only food choices at the store, but also to create political and social alliances with others in an effort to make agroecological food more accessible.

Another way that movements aim to challenge the social and economic forces that shape who can and can't afford certain foods is by supporting the *right to food*. As part of the international human rights discourse, proponents of the right to food argue that being able to access nutritious and culturally appropriate food is a critical component of being able to lead a dignified and flourishing life. As such, food should be de-commodified, or de-coupled from capitalist logics and markets, so that no one is in the position of not being able to afford

The trendy interior of Mercado São Jorge.

healthy foods. In Brazil, social movements and civil society were successful in getting the right to food legally enshrined in the constitution in 2010 — a major achievement — but implementation gaps mean that there is still a long way to go to ensure universal access to good food in practice.

ACOLHIDA NA COLÔNIA: AGRITOURISM

While everyone needs to be guaranteed the right to food, farmers and workers also need to be guaranteed the right to make a good living. Yet, unfortunately, the compensation that farmers across the board receive for their work has been declining. As the price of food has steadily dropped over the past decades while costs of living and production have risen, farmers —especially small-scale farmers — are increasingly pushed to economically diversify in order to make ends meet. Agroecological farmers in Santa Catarina diversify their on-farm production by cultivating various species and crop varieties, integrating crops and animals, and transforming raw foods into value-added products (for instance, making cheese from milk or preserves from fresh produce). They also increasingly diversify their off-farm activities; for example, Cleber took up a position as a councillor at his local prefecture.

Sítio Arroio da Serra (Stream of the Mountains), located in Urubici, is run by Seu Eraldo and Dona Terezinha. This part of the state is well known for its unique geology, waterfalls, and cycling paths.

Guests can stay overnight in small cabanas.

Seu Eraldo and Dona Terezinha produce Rede Ecovida-certified persimmons (pictured here) and kiwi, most of which they sell through a local cooperative.

An on-farm but not directly production-related activity into which agroecological farmers in Santa Catarina are increasingly venturing is agritourism. In particular, there is a well-known agritourism network of *pousadas* (which means "inns," but is closer to what are often called "bed and breakfasts") across the state made up of entirely agroecological farmers, called Acolhida na Colônia.

Acolhida na Colônia's objectives include "improving the quality of life of participating family farmers by organizing agritourism activities as a complementary source of income" and "enhancing the activities of participating family farmers, offering alternatives for them to remain in the countryside, maintaining their history and culture and strengthening an agricultural practice using the principles of agroecology that protect and regenerate the environment."[5]

Through the Acolhida na Colônia network, customers can pay to visit (and often stay overnight at) participating farms in order to (re)connect with nature and directly support the livelihoods of small-scale, agroecological family farmers. For example, if you were to visit Pousada Vítoria, run by Dona Dida and her son, Jackson, you could learn about the history of their region, which used to be heavily characterized by tobacco production but is now informally referred to as the agroecology capital of Santa Catarina. Dona Dida might tell you about the native corn varieties she grows and the traditional corn flour she processes from them, or Jackson might show you the apiary they created in order to support *abelhas nativas* (native bees) — you might even get to sample honey straight from the source. In this way,

Dona Dida owns Pousada Vitória in Santa Rosa de Lima, informally known as the agroecology capital of Santa Catarina. She is showing native varieties of corn, from which she makes homemade farinha (flour).

Dona Dida preparing homemade fritters for guests.

Dona Dida's guest breakfast — homemade cakes, jams and jellies, breads, cheese, and more.

Dona Dida's son, Jackson, showing a guest honey produced by native bees on their farm.

an objective of the network is to "promote the connections between the countryside and the city through the sharing of experiences, and by allowing family farmers to live together with the inhabitants of urban centres."[6]

As Gleissman articulates, this model can play an important role in helping the transition toward a more agroecological food system by "re-establish[ing] a more direct connection between those who grow our food and those who consume it."[7] Forming direct relationships between eaters and growers can lead to a better understanding on the part of the eater in terms of the work and care that farmers put into growing food and stewarding agroecosystems. When enough of these relationships are built, there is a potential for wider, community-scale (or even societal-scale) shifts in beliefs, attitudes, and values around agriculture and food. This could lead to more eaters desiring agroecological foods and pushing for policy incentives and other supports for agroecological farms. In this sense, building stronger rural-urban relationships and alliances is a key factor in scaling out agroecology.

ELAINE AND SÉRGIO: NEO-RURALISM

By Fernando do Espírito Santo, Bachelor of Journalism, Federal University of Santa Catarina

While agrotourism generally allows urban people to take short visits to the countryside, other trends in urban agroecology establish deeper and longer-lasting commitments and relationships with rural places. Sítio Florbela is located on a mountain in the historic village of Sertão do Ribeirão, 30 kilometres from the centre of Florianópolis. The property belongs to a couple, Elaine and Sérgio, who purchased it in 2013. They still live and work in the core of the city a few days a week in order to finance their farm, making them a part of what is known in Brazil as the *neo-rural* movement — people who seek to reconnect with nature and are leaving highly urbanized areas to live in the countryside.

Elaine and Sérgio under a shade cloth with seedlings in preparation for planting.

Elaine's work on the farm is closely linked to her ancestors and her culture. They named the farm after her Aunt Florbela, and Elaine also goes on to say, "my grandfather was a full-fledged farmer and now I am here as the owner of the farm, and we are working on agriculture and environmental education, cultural revitalization, and getting back to the land." Elaine's work also involves the preservation of *sementes crioulas* (heritage seeds) — seeds that are not cultivated or designed for commercial production but instead are saved by farmers and gardeners, sometimes stretching back generations. Elaine attended a seed-saving event and has since been enthralled with preserving this symbol of agroecological identity: "I became passionate about seeds and we greatly strengthened this idea that we are not organic producers; we're agroecological." Elaine sees "organic" and "agroecological" farmers as different: Social, cultural, and often broader ecological relationships are given more priority in agroecological farming in Brazil, whereas organic can refer more narrowly to the specific farming practices that are required to be certified according to the organic standards. As Sérgio explains,

Often, organic agriculture ends up resembling industrial agriculture in the logic of production — for example with the application of pesticides, the difference being that in organic systems you can only use an organic-approved pesticide. But our idea [as agroecological farmers] goes beyond that, we want the health of the plants, to understand the plants, since a healthy plant does not need a pesticide. We look

Workers tending the field at Sitío Florbela.

Sérgio pruning a eucalyptus tree in his agroforestry plot.

for ways of creating systems on our property that give us this possibility of growing a healthy plant, which is better for the whole system.

Before Elaine and Sérgio took over, the farm only had degraded pasture for cattle, which were raised on-site. The former owners used industrial management methods, so when Elaine and Sérgio decided to do something different, the farm had to go through a multi-year transition process. This process requires farmers to cut out use of most agrichemicals and to implement practices that prevent (to the extent possible) their farm from being contaminated by pesticide drift from neighbouring farms, among making other changes.

Among the most impressive of the agroecological experiments happening on Elaine and Sérgio's property is the practice of agroforestry. In agroforestry systems, trees work with other elements of the system, which, like a forest, mature and improve over time, requiring less work while providing good yields and improving soil health.[8]

Other important activities on their farm include raising native stingless bees and reforesting the banks of the local river that winds through their property and leads to the nearby lake, Lagoa do Peri, the main source of water supplying the south of Florianópolis. All of these activities and the decisions that Elaine and Sérgio make at Sítio Florbela relate back to their desire to farm in harmony with nature, to eat and provide healthy food, and to respect and celebrate local culture.

GLAICO: MAKING FOOD AFFORDABLE

In contrast to bringing urban people onto rural farms through agritourism or the neo-rural "back to the land" movement, rural agroecological farmers create and visit markets in urban areas to sell their produce. Take Glaico, who is considered a "reference point" for agroecology in the wider Florianópolis region — when we met him, he had already been farming for twenty-four years (organically for twenty-three of those years). His farm is located in a municipality about an hour's drive outside of the city on a property of just over 7 hectares, much of which he received initially through the Banco da Terra program.

Glaico's property is a bit unique biophysically in that it contains a lot of different soil types that are found across the state, so researchers at local universities frequently conduct research projects on his farm. He currently cultivates around fifty different kinds of crops and manages an agroforestry system. Eventually he plans to integrate chickens and other livestock into his farm as well as aquaculture, outlining plans to expand upon the network of canals he's installed by creating a pond on his property so that he can re-introduce an almost-extinct native species of fish that thrives in standing pools of water.

He's also building an *agroindústria* (processing facility) on his property and eventually would like to host tourists through Acolhida na Colônia. This diversity of activities requires a lot of labour, but he is not able to afford hiring of additional workers (although one of his daughters helps with marketing and sales). He sells his products on his property, where he hosts a small on-farm market, but more importantly, he is the founder of the organic market in the Lagoa da Conceição neighbourhood of Florianópolis, where he also sells his produce.

For a large agroecological transition to happen, there needs to be a market for agroecological

Glacio's farm, not too far from the town of Paulo Lopes.

Some of Glaico's agroecological produce.

products and money in it for people who are going to produce this way. At the same time, many of the farmers who are members of Rede Ecovida or are otherwise involved with the agroecology movement are committed to feeding their local communities — and not just the wealthy. Glaico, for one, is steadfast in his commitment to making the food he grows accessible. Because he sells directly to eaters through the small market on his farm or the larger farmers' market in Florianópolis and does not have to rely on an intermediary to negotiate

Glaico rings up a customer at the organic market he was instrumental in starting in Lagoa da Conceição.

with distributors or retailers — who mark up (sometimes quite significantly) the cost of food in order to make a profit — he is able to price his food in a way that ensures working- and middle-class Brazilians can also afford it. He's not rich (and certainly is not compensated enough for the valuable work he does through farming and community organizing), but he makes ends meet and fulfils his ethical commitment to providing healthy, local foods to everyday people. Luckily, due to the commitment of farmers and organizers like Glaico who have brought healthy, fair food into the public eye, larger groups of consumers have become interested in regularly supporting agroecological farmers and have come together to do so through initiatives like the Responsible Consumer Cells (Células de Consumidores Responsáveis, CCR) network.

RESPONSIBLE CONSUMER CELLS NETWORK

By Isadora Leite Escosteguy and Prof. Oscar José Rover,
Agroecosystems Program, Federal University of Santa Catarina

The Responsible Consumer Cells (CCR) network started as a research project in the Family Farming Commercialization Laboratory at the Federal University of Santa Catarina (LACAF/ UFSC)[9] and in dialogue with national and international researchers. The CCR network is a model of direct sales, where groups of Rede Ecovida farmers are linked to consumer groups (cells) that are interested in supporting them. Through pre-orders, the CCR network aims to create and structure market channels for the purchase and sale of agroecological foods by stimulating ethical and responsible consumption, in order to increase the supply of food from organic family farms in the greater Florianópolis region at affordable prices.

The CCR network works on a closed basket model, where the eater doesn't get to choose which foods will be included in the basket each week. Instead, the farmers provide a variety of foods at a fixed weight and price, and the foods differ according to the farmer's production system and the season. In this way, the CCR network provides an opportunity to change people's eating habits by encouraging them to consume organic foods on a regular basis, while participants also gain knowledge about the seasonality of different foods, which helps eaters diversify their diets and expand their food literacy, or their knowledge and understanding of food and its origins[10] (such as what time of year certain foods can be grown locally, or how

Organizer meeting prior to consumer pick-up for the CCR program.

Examples of CCR *baskets.*

to prepare or use certain fruits, vegetables, herbs, etc.). The baskets are paid for on a monthly basis and delivered weekly. Each basket contains the following items: a) two types of greens, b) one or two types of fruit, c) two types of other vegetables, d) one or two types of roots or tubers, and e) two types of spices and/or teas. There are two different basket models to choose from, at very reasonable prices — a smaller one, with approximately 4.5 kilograms of food (between seven and nine items) at a price of 29 reais (about Can$7), and a larger one, with approximately 9 kilograms of food (between thirteen and fourteen items; the large baskets also include a grain), at a price of 53 reais (about Can$13). In addition to offering closed baskets, groups of farmers have made available a list of additional products for purchase, so that each member can complement their basket with other products if they so choose. Farmers harvest food the day before delivery, and distribution takes place at agreed-upon delivery points accessible to all the consumers in a cell, which can include schools, neighbourhood associations, universities, a member's house, or other locations.

The CCR model responds to family farmers' need for direct markets and provides a financial guarantee to family farmers, since they know in advance which products will be sold and in what quantities. In this sense, farmers have the ability to carry out production and logistics planning in response to an already-defined level of demand, which also helps farmers reduce food losses and waste. On the other hand, for consumers, this arrangement is convenient and provides guaranteed access to healthy and local food. As mentioned in Glaico's story, in this system, there is no distributor intervening to capture profits, which ensures better remuneration for farming families as well as more afford-able prices for consumers. For this reason, initiatives like the CCR program — and the CSA model, which is more familiar in North America — contribute to agroecological transitions by directly linking growers and eaters and expanding the reach of agroecol-ogy in both rural and urban places.

One way in which CCR and CSA programs differ, though, is in the responsibility for coordination. One of the tenets of the CCR initiative is that responsibilities are shared and cells are self-managed. Therefore, each consumer group has its own coordinator, and each farmer group has its own as well. The farmer coordinator is responsible for managing orders and receipts (via bank transfers and deposits) and administering

Isadora, the co-author of this story — and whose master's research focused on the CCR program — holding a CCR basket.

transport. The consumer coordinator handles communication with both the farmer coordina-tor and consumer members, develops collective strategies for administration, and manages the basket delivery points. This consumer coordinator role is a rotating responsibility, so everyone plays a part in supporting their cell.

The CCR project started in November 2017 with one group of farmers providing one con-sumer cell with twenty-seven baskets. Today there are six groups of farmers (representing approximately sixty families) providing twelve cells with about 400 baskets per week (equat-ing to more than 7 tonnes of food per month), with a hundred consumers on the waiting list to join the program.

The CCR network provides an opportunity for collective change by bringing together grow-ers and eaters and encouraging the engagement of urban people, highlighting the important role that the active eater-citizen can play in democratizing food systems.[11,12]

TÂNEA: CO-FARMERS SUPPORTING FARMERS

This brings us to Tânea, another fixture in the agroecology movement in Santa Catarina and the coordinator of a Rede Ecovida *nucleo*. Tânea runs a mixed vegetable farm with her partner, Vitor, and sells their produce to members of her CCR. She was three years into a five-year lease on the land that she was farming when we went to visit her. However, she had identified a more permanent option nearby with a little more land — she needed more space because she had already reached capacity for her CCR members. She would need some time to transition from one property to the next, so in the fifth year of her rental arrangement she was planning to farm both properties.

A necessary component of the transition toward agroecology for rural producers involves finding a stable land tenure arrangement. Renting land can be challenging for agroecological farmers for a number of reasons. First, it takes time to certify as organic, so leases need to be at least a few years long. It also requires farmers to invest labour and resources, which do not necessarily pay off in the short term, especially since they need to wait to benefit from the price premium.

Tânea and Vitor have some help in carrying out all of the work on the farm thanks to the labour of their customers. In fact, Tânea's philosophy toward farming and her customers departs markedly from the language of "consumer," and even of "eater." As she puts it:

> It's not that we want to produce organic food to offer to people. This is not our goal;
> we want to provide healthy food, but the goal is to bring people closer to reality, you

Tânea speaking at the plenary during a Rede Ecovida regional nucleo *meeting.*

Tânea harvesting some strawberries.

Co-farmers learning how to identify weeds and pests.

An agroecological co-farmer travelling home after a long day on Tânea's farm.

know? To construct agroecology like this so that people understand what it's like to be outside of the city, to understand where their food comes from. We have the agroecological food, but that is not the goal. It's the construction itself, and bringing farmers and co-farmers here.

Tânea and Vitor gave their CCR members the label of "co-farmers" to recognize their role in the farmer-eater relationship and to try to challenge the assumption that they were merely passive consumers. Rather, co-farmers have a role to play in the production of agroecological food — they participate in the agroecological transition, too. For Tânea, this is more than semantics. Regularly over the course of the growing season, co-farmers would leave Florianópolis for a farm visit and would work alongside Tânea in the field, tending to the fruits, vegetables, and chickens.

Tânea's CCR members share in the agroecological labour as well as enjoy the fruits of that labour. This relationship has helped bring more urban people out to the country and to connect them with the land and the people that provide them with sustenance.

GROWING FOOD IN URBAN PLACES

By Erika Sagae, Vice President of CEPAGRO

Agroecology doesn't just happen on farms in the countryside; urban people can practise agroecology in the heart of the city, too. CEPAGRO has been working with urban agriculture for a long time, supporting and raising awareness around community composting initiatives and urban gardens. In addition, CEPAGRO encourages urban people to consider their role in the food system in both rural and urban areas. It's important for the eater to understand that the act of consuming is not restricted to only buying food. We should also understand how it was produced, how much it costs to reach the city, and how to organize to support farmers.

CEPAGRO considers it essential to be active in political spaces, such as policy fora, councils, and community networks, in order to build public policies consistent with real-life experiences. For instance, CEPAGRO participates in Rede Semear (Seeding Network), which is composed of various stakeholders that participate in urban agriculture, including representatives of NGOs, urban farmers and gardeners, and public institutions (such as those responsible for waste management, parks, education, and health). Since 2015, Rede Semear has been

Two CEPAGRO *affiliates sharing their work on urban composting and educating passersby at the Extension Education Week at the Federal University of Santa Catarina.*

meeting and hosting gatherings, producing a critical mass of supporters that advocate for local policies that support urban agriculture and agroecology in the city, such as the 2017 municipal decree that established a citywide urban agriculture program.

Other municipal decrees and policies have recently been approved that aim to create, integrate, and adapt municipal policies and programs to encourage agroecology. For one, Law 10,501/2019 requires organic material to be recycled and composted, and Law 10,628/2019 establishes and defines agricultural and livestock production areas as well as areas used for *extrativismo* as pesticide-free zones in the municipality of Florianópolis.

Florianópolis stands out regionally and nationally because — beyond being partially located on an island — it is a capital city that still has a rural character. It is possible to stroll through some neighbourhoods of the city and see horses and oxen, having escaped from nearby suburban paddocks where they graze, walking down the street.

Community gardens such as Horta do PACUCA (Parque Cultural do Campeche), which is located in the Campeche Cultural Park (a historical and cultural heritage site), are often

Cattle roam the streets of Lagoa da Conceição, one of the neighbourhoods in Florianópolis most popular with tourists. Even though it is a densely populated urban neighbourhood, it still has green space grazed by livestock.

The PACUCA Community Garden. In the middle of the right-hand side, you can see the garden beds, which, from above, resemble an airplane, commemorating the fact that the area used to be an aviation field (with famous French author Antoine de Saint-Exupéry even having landed there while working as a pilot in the 1920s–30s).

A Cultive sign (translation: "cultivate" or "grow") at the PACUCA Community Garden.

the site of struggle over community access to public lands. But their value to local people is clear: During the COVID-19 crisis, for example, PACUCA has strengthened the Campeche neighbourhood because a large part of what has been produced in the garden has been donated to families in need and to soup kitchens that are providing free meals.

These are just some examples that describe how people and institutions are rethinking what cities should be, and how food should be produced, at a very local level. Agroecology is really important in this sense because urban agriculture can provide an entry point for building relationships of care with the environment and by demonstrating the various parts of the food cycle, from composting to production to consumption (and back again).

REVOLUÇÃO DOS BALDINHOS

Managing food waste through composting has played an important role in the neighbourhood of Chico Mendes, located in a working-class and more informal part of Florianópolis. Chico Mendes is on the continental side of the city, which sits across a thin stretch of Atlantic Ocean that divides the much greener and more rural island-based part of the city from the highly urbanized portion that spills over onto the mainland.

In 2008, a leptospirosis outbreak tragically killed two community members in Chico Mendes. The outbreak occurred due to an absence of municipal waste collection; food waste built up in the streets, which led to a rat infestation, with rats being the disease vectors of leptospirosis. In response to the threat the rats posed, a group of community members, led by two women named Cintia and Karol, started to organize to address the problem. The resulting Revolução dos Baldinhos (Bucket Revolution) started with a few founding organizers going door-to-door to raise awareness about the problem of food waste in the streets and to

The bridge to the continental side of Florianópolis from the perspective of the more forested, island-based part of the city.

Outside the headquarters of the Revolução dos Baldinhos in Chico Mendes.

introduce composting as a solution. Composting is the process of working with microbes, invertebrates, and insects to speed up the decomposition of food waste and transform it into nutrient-rich soil.

Neighbours started to accept their proposal and collected their kitchen scraps, which

Cintia and Karol, two of the main leaders of the Revolução dos Baldinhos, hosting a composting workshop.

At a community composting pátio *build in the Chico Mendes neighbourhood, Julio from* CEPAGRO, *moves some straw in a tarp to build the pátio.*

Later, Revolução dos Baldinhos co-founder Cintia filled it with compost with some help from a community member.

were then picked up in wagons and taken to community compost *pátios* (or yards), where they were tended. Within a matter of months, the compost was ready for use to grow healthy vegetables or sell as fertilizer to support the project. This whole arrangement was managed entirely by the community in the absence of a centralized municipal composting program.

The project is called a "social technology" that is easily shared with other communities;

Karol, after speaking with university students during a composting workshop.

in fact, it has already spread across the country. Due to its remarkable success, the group won an international prize in the category of "Outstanding Practices in Agroecology" from the World Future Council in recognition of its contribution not only to the Chico Mendes community, but to the wider agroecology movement.

Urban composting initiatives are crucial for closing the metabolic rift — the disconnect in the cycle of nutrients between the city and the country. Farmers in the countryside grow food, which is then shipped into cities to be consumed by urban people, eventually making its way into the sewer system or being discarded as waste. Since agricultural soils are not an endless source of these nutrients, cities need to recycle those nutrients back into agricultural soils. This is exactly what the Revolução dos Baldinhos (Bucket Revolution) does. Not only does the food waste stop attracting pests (like disease-carrying rats) and get turned into valuable organic matter that can increase soil fertility in the form of compost, it also creates a potential revenue stream for the communities doing the composting, who, in this case, had been neglected and unsupported by formal programming, in large part due to class- and race-based prejudice. Initiatives like this not only help to close the metabolic rift by returning nutrients consumed by urban people back to agricultural soils, but they also provide examples of how community care and

Compost in the making at a composting workshop hosted by CEPAGRO *and colleagues.*

locally led efforts can call attention to the need for more structural changes that support environmental justice and social equity.

Building deeper rural–urban relationships and a sense of solidarity is crucial for advancing food-systems transformation based on agroecology. As it currently stands, some of these relationships are limited to market transactions, or "voting with your fork." Because industrial "food from nowhere" typically costs less for consumers while people who seek out agroecological foods may have to pay a premium, agroecological foods are in some cases only accessible to those with social and economic privilege. However, alternative market spaces are intentionally being set up to make agroecological foods more accessible and affordable — take the Lagoa market founded by Glaico, for example. In addition, emerging responsible consumer networks are another way in which eaters can build long-term, supportive, and fair relationships with farmers.

In addition to market-based transactions, other kinds of relationships are being forged between urban people and the people and lands that grow agroecological food. Agritourism initiatives and co-farmer visits are important since they provide a vehicle for bringing people from the city out to the countryside, to better understand the energy, effort, and resources that go into growing agroecological food. Perhaps these kinds of experiences can inspire urban people to explore the possibility of moving to rural places to experiment with a land-based, neo-rural lifestyle, as Elaine and Sérgio are doing. Lastly, urban agroecological initiatives promise to help close the metabolic rift through community-based urban composting programs (where food is transformed back into productive and healthy soil in the city) and municipal policies that support urban farms and gardens (closing the knowledge rift and supplying agroecological foods directly to city residents).

Chapter 5

ENVISIONING THE FUTURE OF AGROECOLOGICAL FOOD SYSTEMS

Transitioning to agroecology from an industrial food system requires both "sustainable farm-scale agroecosystems" and "new relationships of sustainability" (Levels 3 and 4).[1] But these steps must also come together to form part of a broader transition toward a food system "based on equity, participation, democracy, and justice, that is not only sustainable but helps restore and protect earth's life support systems upon which we all depend" (Level 5).[2] So how do the examples shared here — of agroecology in action at the local and regional levels (Levels 2, 3, and 4) — relate to broader food-systems transitions (Level 5)?

Broader change in the food system requires changing not only how we produce and consume food but also the way people live in relation to others and the land: it is about reducing inequality by shifting how resources and power are allocated in the food system. This view of agroecology is sometimes called "political agroecology"[3] because it highlights the need to address the root causes of inequities in the food system that perpetuate social and ecological harm.[4] Some of those inequities run between older and younger generations; others cut across lines of race, class, and gender; others still relate to struggles over Indigenous lands, just to name a few. These are some of the political issues that agroecology movements, in Brazil and elsewhere, have to confront.

"WITHOUT YOUTH, THERE IS NO AGROECOLOGY!"

At agroecological events and protests, it's not uncommon to hear chants of *Sem juventude, não há agroecologia!* ("Without youth, there is no agroecology!"). This slogan calls attention to a major challenge for agroecology and agriculture more generally — what has been called the "generation problem."[5] In many countries around the world, the average age of farmers is increasing. In Brazil, nearly half of all farmers are age 55 or older.[6] Brazil has also urbanized dramatically over the past few decades, with many people having left the countryside in the rural exodus, to live and work in cities. This trend, sometimes also called "depeasantization,"[7]

Young farmers Luana and Jorel with native corn varieties.

raises critical questions about the future of farming. As Luana and Jorel, a young farming couple, describe:

> Jorel: We see that there are no new, young people. There are a lot of older people, more experienced people.

> Luana: Who will take care of the fields in the future, right, if there are only older people?

In other words, given the aging farming population and increasing urbanization, who will be the next generation of (agroecological) farmers?

While the average age of farmers might be increasing, the agroecology movement has a distinctly youthful character. Take Luana and Jorel — they met while attending a local university to study chemistry (Jorel) and agroecology (Luana). When we met them they were renting a 3-hectare farm property on the outskirts of Lages, a mid-sized city in the south-central part of Santa Catarina, in the PSC. The outskirts of the city, or the regions around or near cities that grow food, are often referred to as peri-urban agricultural areas. They are critical for a number of reasons: for one, with sufficient protection from development pressures they can

Jorel feeding the hens while Luana watches.

help halt urban sprawl from encroaching on agricultural land or sensitive ecosystems. They also provide cities with access to local food, increasing the self-sufficiency of both the city and the surrounding countryside through the development of "city-regional food systems."[8] In addition, peri-urban areas can increase the interaction of urban people with the process of growing food, thereby increasing food literacy. Finally, they offer farmers — new farmers and young farmers in particular — easy access to urban services, markets, and opportunities.

Having grown up with the internet and social media, Luana and Jorel have both been using online platforms to connect with local eaters and share more about their farming philosophy. Through their participation in Rede Ecovida, they have been able to support other agroecological farmers who are less social-media savvy, don't have regular access to the internet, or are in remote rural areas by picking up those farmers' goods and including them in their own weekly CSA program and deliveries. Many of the Rede Ecovida farmers we met described the benefits of working together by bringing their respective knowledges and experiences to the table, and forming supportive and reciprocal relationships. Speaking to the spirit of collaboration, rather than competition, that is so central to Rede Ecovida's success, Luana says:

Jorel and Luana's farm, on the outskirts of Lages.

As we are a part of a Rede Ecovida group of farmers, we partner with those in our group and sell some products from them, because they are older people and they live farther out in the countryside. So, they don't have much access to information or to social media to do any dissemination and marketing … And the internet is a very good way to do that. It is something that is working [for us].

While young people who grew up in the countryside have been leaving agriculture over the past few decades in search of educational opportunities and higher-paying jobs in cities, agroecology has provided a new pathway for youth who want to find work that is challenging, rewarding, creative, and connects them to nature. For example, Luana and Jorel won an award in a university competition for "technology, entrepreneurship, and innovation" because of their willingness to experiment and persevere in transforming the degraded pastureland they are renting into a farm based on agroecological principles. For these reasons, young people around the world are at the forefront of advancing strategies that promote sustainable food systems.[9]

"WITHOUT FEMINISM, THERE IS NO AGROECOLOGY!"

Beyond generational inequities, the agrifood system is rife with gender inequities. When it comes to farming, gendered labour roles often lead to men controlling decisions about farm management, marketing, commercialization of farm products, and income, whereas women are often responsible for reproductive labour in the home and in the fields — gardening, seed-saving, cooking, cleaning, raising children, and other domestic chores.[10]

Agroecology, as a way of changing farming relations, aims to bring about greater gender equality. Feminism has played an increasingly prominent role in agroecology movements in Brazil, as evidenced by another slogan popularized at the National Meetings of Agroecology organized by Brazil's National Agroecology Alliance (Articulação Nacional de Agroecologia, ANA): *Sem feminismo, não há agroecologia!* ("Without feminism, there is no agroecology!").[11] From conferences in the city (such as the Agroecological Festival in Florianópolis) to the festivals in the countryside (like the Pinhão Festival in the PSC), women in the agroecology movement are taking a stand for more equitable gender relations and emphasizing the important role that women have played as protagonists in the agroecology movement.

An important social movement in this respect is the Rural Women's Movement (Movimento de Mulheres Camponesas, MMC), which began in southern Brazil and which has strong roots in Santa Catarina in particular. Members of the MMC have played a crucial role in bringing

Tânea, the Rede Ecovida coordinator, speaks on a panel on Women and Agroecology at a seminar in Florianópolis. She's standing next to Karol, from Revolucão dos Baldinhos.

Closing ceremony at the Women and Agroecology seminar.

Centro Vianei organizer Carol speaking about the importance of women in agroecology at the Pinhão Festival in the PSC.

MMC *member Joana inspects some transplants on her farm.*

discussions on women's empowerment into agroecological spaces. According to the MMC's website, they started organizing to promote rural women's liberation and empowerment:

> Because we want to stay in the countryside, producing food, preserving life, species and nature, developing a democratic project for agriculture through: agroecology, preserving biodiversity, using medicinal plants, saving seeds in the service of humanity, growing healthy food for the food sovereignty of nations, diversification of production, and appreciation of the work of peasant women ... because we, peasant women, have the capacity to decide and direct our own actions; we have the necessary knowledge, obtained by the experience of confronting the neoliberal model that produces simultaneous gender oppression and class exploitation that injures the dignity of women and men, young and old, black, white and Indigenous ... our activism is a seedbed in the process of recovery and construction of new relationships, values and principles.[12]

Political agroecology, as an effort to counter unequal relations in the food system, is therefore also a feminist project. To echo the words of scholar Rachel Bezner Kerr, "without addressing gender and other social inequities, and developing new forms of organization that address injustice, agroecology is simply an environmentally-friendly way of farming."[13]

"IF THERE IS RACISM, THERE IS NO AGROECOLOGY!"

Political agroecology depends on bringing diverse social groups — youth, women, unions, rural workers, researchers, progressive policymakers, white settler farmers, Afro-Brazilians, Indigenous Peoples, other traditional populations, and more — together to unite in a shared struggle against industrial agriculture and to chart a course forward. Part of building solidarity across diverse groups of people is acknowledging and respecting social difference, including racial and ethnic difference. To this end, the agroecology movement also recognizes that *Se tem racismo, não há agroecologia!* ("If there is racism, there is no agroecology!").[14]

Indigenous Peoples have lived throughout what has been territorialized as Brazil since time immemorial. When the Portuguese invaded in 1500, they began the (still ongoing) colonization of Indigenous lands and the dispossession of Indigenous Peoples from their traditional territories. Brazil's drastic land inequality is rooted in the colonial period, when the Portuguese monarchy divided Brazil into fourteen captaincies, which were presided over by twelve grantees — members of the Portuguese elite.[15] Today, Indigenous reserves in Brazil currently comprise only about 14 percent of the land base, with virtually all of this land located in the Amazon rainforest.[16] Further, the current president of Brazil, Jair Bolsonaro, stated during his campaign in 2017: "*Não vai ter um centímetro demarcado para reserva indígena ou para quilombola*" ("There won't be one centimetre more demarcated for Indigenous reserves or Afro-Brazilian communities").[17] Bolsonaro's intent has been to open up more land for extractive development, particularly for agribusiness interests. He has even attempted to transfer the responsibilities of the Fundação Nacional do Índio (FUNAI, Brazil's national Indigenous affairs body) to the Ministry of Agriculture, Livestock, and Supply (MAPA) — a state agency whose leadership has a vested interest in enclosing and privatizing Indigenous and public lands for agribusiness interests.

Members of the Kaingang community march in protest of inadequate housing in Florianópolis.

In the end, Bolsonaro's attempt to

transfer the responsibility to demarcate Indigenous lands to MAPA was overturned by the Supreme Court. Nonetheless, the Bolsonaro administration has continued to undermine Indigenous self-determination in Brazil while land invasions, deforestation, and violence against Indigenous Peoples continue to grow.[18] In the Amazon, Indigenous land defenders now have to additionally contend with the fact that invasions by loggers, miners, and ranchers are bringing COVID-19 into their territories, where they have extremely limited access to health care.[19]

Despite these major setbacks in Brazilian national policy that undermine Indigenous and environmental rights, the agroecology movement recently released a political charter on "Land, Territory, Diversity, and Struggles" that affirms the movement's commitment to centre marginalized communities and cooperate "to build a new project for the countryside."[20]

While this commitment is welcome, Kaingang leader Douglas Jacinto da Rosa has raised the need to consider the ways in which Indigenous worldviews are distinct from those held by non-Indigenous people in the wider agroecology movement:

> It is necessary to … discuss this powerful and creative counterpoint that is agroecology. But these concepts need to be refined, as Indigenous practices and knowledge [include] much broader, immemorial traditions. The first step toward agroecology is the immediate reclamation of the demarcation of [Indigenous] lands.[21]

Jacinto da Rosa's remarks highlight how land is central to Indigenous Peoples' ways of living and being in the world. As seen in the following example of Tekoá V'ya, land is crucial for building Indigenous food sovereignty, or the reclamation of traditional and culturally important foods and lifeways for Indigenous Peoples.

TEKOÁ V'YA: ENACTING INDIGENOUS FOOD SOVEREIGNTY

By Charles (Bagé) Lamb, Rural Programs Coordinator, CEPAGRO

Located 120 kilometres outside of Florianópolis, Tekoá V'ya is a Guaraní community with 160 hectares of reserve land, made up of a mix of forest, agriculture, and housing facilities. This land was redistributed to the community by the state, as they were displaced from their original settlement due to the negative environmental effects caused by the construction of a federal highway. So, the community has been in this specific territory, which they've named Aldeia Feliz (Happy Reserve), since 2009. Initially, there were just fifteen families, but the community has since grown to forty-four families in total (about 170 people).

Agriculture is at the core of the Guaraní/Mbyá culture, kept alive through songs, religious ceremonies, and the worldview transmitted to each new generation through experience and language. Tekoá V'ya has gardens, collective and family cropland, and a traditional Guaraní school with elementary education, as well as programs for teaching youth and adults. The

Children in the Tekoá V'ya community play outside a traditional school.

Corn and other crops growing at Tekoá V'ya.

community also receives Indigenous families from different Brazilian states on exchange visits, bringing other agricultural experiences and questions about various practices into the community.

Agriculture in Tekoá V'ya uses unique adaptations in response to the soil and climatic conditions, which are different from the surrounding region. The community grows a sequence of crops, including fruits, roots, and tubers, and annual crops, and brings in varieties from outside through exchanges between *parentes* (relatives or kin, often broader than western notions of the family).

The transmission of oral histories, passed on mainly by elders, is paramount to carry forward the cultural history and knowledge of traditional foods for future generations. The central traditional food is the Guaraní corn, called *avaxi ete'i*, which is maintained from generation to generation. It is used in many traditional ceremonies, including to perform children's baptisms, and when a family moves between *aldeias*, they always bring traditional corn seeds with them.

The actions of public agencies and NGOs with Tekoá V'ya have been aimed at supporting food security for families by working with agroecological management techniques, facilitating access to seedlings of perennial fruit species, and providing access to varieties of vegetables and other foods that not only increase the diversity of foods available but also respect Guaraní/Mbyá food traditions. Fundamental for the next generations of Guaraní — and for the maintenance, strength, and well-being of the current generations — is being able to enact Indigenous food sovereignty through having access to diverse foods, speaking their language, and having the ability to carry out ceremonial aspects of their culture, even when located outside of their traditional home territories.

"AGROECOLOGY AND DEMOCRACY ARE UNITING CITY AND COUNTRY"

As we have tried to highlight throughout this book, agroecology is not only a science and practice, but also a social movement. One of the first things that likely comes to mind when thinking of a social movement is public protest — thousands of people in the streets, demanding social change. As is the case with many Latin American countries, Brazil has a vibrant and rich but also sombre history of social movement struggles. The fight for collective rights, such as the right to land, is at the very heart of politics in the country. Since the Green Revolution began, Brazil has undergone a number of political transformations, the major one being the transition back to democracy after the twenty-year-long military dictatorship that ended in the mid-1980s. As social movement pressures built in the 1980s during the period of re-democratization — and despite the pressures of neoliberalism — some progressive and influential ideas were included in the country's 1988 constitution and instituted by presidential administrations, most notably the Lula administration (2003–2010). For example, in this book we touch on the importance of public procurement programs, like the National School Lunch Program (PNAE). While PNAE has existed for decades, in 2009, the Lula administration expanded its mandate to link family farmers to stable, local markets and to provide an incentive for transitioning toward agroecological production (because certified farmers receive a price premium through the program). Another example is the approval by Brazil's Congress in 2010 of a constitutional amendment to explicitly include recognition of the state's obligation to guarantee the right to food. Law and policy innovations such as these have not only propelled Brazil into a position of global leadership in the realms of food security and agroecology, but they also have had tangible impacts on the lives of millions of people living there, lifting many out of hunger and poverty.

Yet more recently, Brazil has faced additional political challenges. In 2016, Lula's successor, Dilma Rousseff, was ousted from office in what is regarded by many public officials and intellectuals as a parliamentary coup, while former president Lula was imprisoned for allegedly accepting bribes during the corruption scandal known as Operacão Lava Jato ("Operation Car Wash"). Under the subsequent Michel Temer administration, and especially under the present Bolsonaro administration, institutional advances related to human rights and the environment have been rolled back. For instance, one of Bolsonaro's first acts upon taking office as president was to introduce Provisional Measure 870, which extinguished the National Council on Food and Nutritional Security (Conselho Nacional de Segurança Alimentar e Nutricional, CONSEA), the organizational body responsible for providing policy recommendations directly to the administration on how to achieve food security and nutrition goals.[22] Importantly and uniquely, CONSEA was composed of one-third government officials and two-thirds civil society actors, acting as a participatory mechanism that allowed civil society to have a direct say in policymaking.[23] Many of the progressive policy mechanisms mentioned above came about due to the recommendations of CONSEA, which has been held up around the world as a successful institutional innovation in the democratization of food policy.[24]

Bolsonaro's presidency is part of a recent, global surge in *authoritarian populism*. Authoritarian populism refers to right-wing appeals to "the people" against supposedly "out-of-touch" political elites. Yet, the policy proposals from authoritarian leaders are not actually in the interest of "the people" — instead, they centralize power by restricting democracy in the interest of corporate elites, ultimately leading to an assault on human health, ecological sustainability, and overall well-being. In Brazil, the alliance between authoritarian leadership and agribusiness is clear: pesticide use has increased to the benefit of transnational agrichemical corporations; democratic spaces for deliberating food policy have been extinguished;[25] and rainforests have been cleared to produce yet more soy and beef — largely for export, but at great cost to local people and the environment.[26]

A range of policymakers, civil society actors, and social movements strongly condemned the eradication of CONSEA — which was perceived as a direct move toward authoritarianism[27] — and were quick to mobilize in opposition. These groups organized a nationwide protest,

An attendee adds some food to a banana leaf plate at Banquetaço.

called Banquetaço ("Large Feast"), centred around a huge public feast in order to draw attention to the importance of CONSEA's role in promoting food security and the right to food. In the words of a key leader from a civil society organization in Brazil that advocates for agroecology and the right to food,

> Not only have policies on food security and agroecology been reversed, there has also been a serious dismantling of environmental and land legislation, and with these barriers created by these changes in the law it makes it impossible to produce agroecologically … So the fight is on several fronts. That is why Banquetaço was a significant moment, especially where farmers and consumers were

CEPAGRO affiliate Juliana serves up a plate to an attendee.

The food pavilion was decorated with plates and colourful political messages about family farming, Indigenous rights, health, and school food (among others) as part of the effort to save CONSEA.

able to bring together the population that is hungry on the street, and young people, there is also a young population living on the street. We need society to understand the broader meaning of food and to understand that eating is a political act. That was a slogan at Banquetaço. Food is a right and not a commodity.

Despite the Banquetaço campaign and other mobilizations, CONSEA did not survive. With such important national-level bodies and policies being dismantled, the need for local-level efforts is greater than ever. One important local leader for the agroecology movement in Florianópolis is Marcos José de Abreu, or Marquito, as he is affectionately known in the city.

When we arrived in Florianópolis, we were told that if we wanted to learn about agroecology in the city, we would need to talk to Marquito — a charismatic city councillor who has the words "Agroecological Space" painted on the wall of his office at City Hall. He got his start as a leader in the movement while writing his thesis about the Revolução dos Baldinhos (Bucket Revolution) and through his work with CEPAGRO. Marquito has been a vocal advocate for agroecology in Florianópolis, advancing policies and programs on composting and community gardens and otherwise ardently promoting agroecological networks across the

City councillor Marquito addresses the crowd at Banquetaço.

An "Out (with) Bolsonaro, freedom and struggle" banner at a protest in downtown Florianópolis.

wider region. He has been a driving force of agroecology-oriented municipal legislation and is seen by many in the movement as an important changemaker — as a person through whom agroecology can make its way onto the mainstream agenda via the political system. This avenue for "political agroecology" is important for agroecological transitions, as it presents a way to scale up agroecological food systems by getting "from protest to policy"[28] at various geographic scales and levels of governance. In other words, *agroecologia e democracia unindo campo e cidade* ("agroecology and democracy are uniting city and country").[29]

So, while the dismantling of food security, nutrition, environmental, and human rights legislation and policy at the national level presents a major challenge for the agroecology movement, *a luta continua* ("the struggle goes on"). The pushback against the Bolsonaro government is part of the ongoing struggle for democracy, food sovereignty, and agroecology in Brazil — a struggle led by civil society that has long railed against the broader structures that prop up the industrial food system, and the corporate and state actors that enable it.

TOWARD A NETWORK OF AGROECOLOGICAL "REAL UTOPIAS"

Just as agroecological farms are resilient, the agroecology movement and the people that comprise it are, too. The spread of authoritarianism,[30] deepening inequality, and the COVID-19 crisis may all represent challenges in the struggle for a transition to just and sustainable food systems based on agroecology, but many of the people featured in this book continue to carry on with bringing agroecology to life, acting as a network of "real utopias" — or at the very least, "waystations" that "concretely demonstrate the virtues of the fuller programme of transformation" and "enhance the capacity for action of people, increasing their ability to push further in the future."[31]

A key element of envisioning real utopias is to understand not only the problems with the world as it currently exists but also to propose possible alternatives that are rooted in everyday structures and conditions (to address real and immediate problems) while also remaining imaginatively ambitious (to encourage people to continue to push for bolder changes). This helps to frame discussions on food systems in transition since it allows us to shine a light on efforts happening across Levels 1–4 of food-systems change in the pursuit of transformative and sustainable food systems "based on equity, participation, democracy, and justice" (Level 5).[32]

We know that the conditions of industrial agriculture are ultimately unsustainable; the agroecology movement in southern Brazil provides examples across Levels 1–4 of the agro-ecological transition that can serve as guidance. These examples include developing farmer-led networks rooted in participatory and egalitarian principles; reducing agrichemical use and negative health effects by transitioning from industrial to diversified organic farming systems; creating new and alternative markets that encourage urban people to connect with rural farmers; enacting community-based solutions to public health problems in the absence of government leadership; reclaiming land and traditional food practices and knowledge; and fighting for policies that simultaneously support small-scale family farmers and provide healthy foods to local communities. All of these examples help us to envision possibilities for a networked, large-scale agroecological transformation (Level 5), while also training us to witness and support those small-scale innovations that are already happening in our own communities — encouraging us to celebrate the people and places that are at the forefront of cultivating real utopias.

LESSONS FROM BRAZIL'S AGROECOLOGICAL UTOPIAS

While we realize that some of the farming practices that are employed by farmers in Brazil may not be applicable to other places, we hope we have made the case that Brazil is a unique and special place to learn about agroecology and its principles. Small-scale farmers, landless peasants, rural workers, women, youth, Indigenous Peoples, and traditional populations in Brazil have long been leading the way in creating more sustainable and just food systems, and they continue to be leaders in moving the needle away from industrial agriculture through their commitment to cultivating real utopias. While agroecology is not a one-size-fits-all model for food-systems change, the principles — such as resisting corporate control, working with nature, developing networks and shared responsibilities, creating spaces for urban agroecology, empowering women and youth, supporting Indigenous food sovereignty, and building solidarity across difference through accountable relationships — can in many ways be translated into different contexts. Through a *diálogo de saberes*[33] (dialogue of knowledges) with people who have other realities and experiences, these principles can be transformed and applied in new sites of struggle against industrial agriculture and in the transition to food systems based on agroecology.

In places such as Canada, there are organizations working to change the food system in ways that are similar to groups like Rede Ecovida, CEPAGRO, and Centro Vianei in Brazil. For instance, the National Farmers Union (a founding member of LVC) and Food Secure Canada work at the national level to push for policy change, while other initiatives are more place-based, such as the Working Group on Indigenous Food Sovereignty (based in Coast and Interior Salish territories in the west) and Union Paysanne (in Québec). And across the country there has been a proliferation of community-led efforts, rooted in the principles of agroecology, that are contributing to more sustainable and just food systems close to home.

There are still many questions that remain for how to scale agroecology up (in policy) and out (across farm sizes, production systems, and geographies). Yet one thing is certain: the negative externalities of the industrial food system are surpassing the planet's capacity to absorb them. This has thrown the food system's resilience into question in an era of resource shortages and an unstable climate. While there will be a number of proposals for a reconfiguration of the food system in the coming years, food-systems transitions should be guided by agroecological examples of real utopias, which aim to improve equity and diversity — and therefore, resilience — in the face of changing conditions. These transitions could be bolstered by a number of policy supports, including increased funding for agroecological research and the redirection of public investment and agricultural subsidies toward agroecological food systems. It also calls for large-scale redistributive policies to ensure that farmers and workers who want to grow agroecological foods have the tools they need to do so and that eaters of all backgrounds are able to access those foods — especially those most in need.

Lastly, it is important to recognize that the shift to agroecology will require a radical reorganizing of food systems that could lead to many benefits but also important losses. An agroecological transition must therefore be a *just transition* — one that provides a safety net for people whose livelihoods are put at risk because of the shift to new practices, technologies, and institutions. Just as small-scale, agroecological farmers often struggle financially, many farmers who have currently invested in industrial agriculture due to the constraints of the global, corporate food regime are also having trouble making ends meet. Therefore, the shift to agroecology will depend both on directly supporting agroecological farmers and on building pathways for conventional farmers and people who otherwise depend on the industrial food system to be a part of the transition.

While the science, practice, and social movement of agroecology give rise to much optimism, the outlook is still tenuous. The future of food is deeply political. Agroecological transitions must always contend with historical and ongoing social and economic inequities throughout the food system as part of building a sustainable future for all.

NOTES

Acknowledgements

1. The research activities took place between October 2017 and May 2019 and were covered under two approved UBC Behavioural Research Ethics Board certificates. We followed the norms established by UBC, CEPAGRO, and Centro Vianei.

Preface

1. Martínez-Torres, M.E., & Rosset, P.M. (2014). Diálogo De Saberes in La Vía Campesina: Food Sovereignty and Agroecology. *Journal of Peasant Studies, 41*(6): 1–20. <https://doi.org/10.1080/03066150.2013. 872632>; Rosset, P.M., Barbosa, L.P., Val, V., & McCune, N. (2020). Pensamiento Latinoamericano Agroecológico: The Emergence of a Critical Latin American Agroecology? *Agroecology and Sustainable Food Systems, 45*(1): 42–64. <https://doi.org/10.1080/21683565.2020.1789908>.
2. We acknowledge that "Canada" and "Brazil" are settler-colonial states and also colonial place names; they are therefore highly contested.
3. Some Indigenous Peoples refer to North America as Turtle Island, reflecting an important creation story. Our use of the place name Turtle Island also challenges the constructs and jurisdictions of the settler states of Canada and the United States, as they occupy Indigenous lands.
4. To pay tribute to this collaboration and facilitate this *diálogo de saberes* between different parts of the global agroecology movement, we have made this book available in both English and Portuguese.

Chapter 1

1. HLPE. (2020). *Impacts of COVID-19 on Food Security and Nutrition: Developing Effective Policy Responses to Address the Hunger and Malnutrition Pandemic.* Rome; Laborde, B.D., Martin, W., Swinnen, J., & Vos, R. (2020). COVID-19 Risks to Global Food Security. *Science, 369*(6503).
2. FSIN. (2021). *Global Report on Food Crises.* <https://www.wfp.org/publications/global-report-food-c rises-2021>.
3. FAO. (2011). *"Energy-Smart" Food for People and Climate.* <http://www.fao.org/3/i2454e/i2454e.pdf>; Usubiaga-Liaño, A., Behrens, P., & Daioglou, V. (2020). Energy Use in the Global Food System. *Journal of Industrial Ecology, 24*(4).
4. FAO. (2019). *The State of Food and Agriculture 2019. Moving Forward on Food Loss and Waste Reduction.* Rome. <http://www.fao.org/3/ca6030en/ca6030en.pdf>; UNEP. (2021). *UNEP Food Waste Index Report*

2021. <https://www.unep.org/resources/report/unep-food-waste-index-report-2021>.

5. Hendrickson, M.K., Howard, P.H., Miller, E.M., & Constance, D.H. (2020). *The Food System: Concentration and Its Impacts.* Family Farm action Alliance. <https://farmactionalliance.org/wp-content/uploads/2020/11/Hendrickson-et-al.-2020.-Concentration-and-Its-Impacts-FINAL.pdf>.

6. Hendrickson, M.K., et al. *The Food System.*

7. Harvey, D. (2005). *A Brief History of Neoliberalism.* Oxford University Press.

8. Ritzer, G. (1996). *The McDonaldization of Society: An Investigation into the Changing Character of Contemporary Social Life.* Thousand Oaks, CA: Pine Forge Press.

9. For a summary of how rationalization informs McDonaldization, see Ritzer, G. (2013). The Weberian Theory of Rationalization and the McDonaldization of Contemporary Society, p. 29–50 in Kivisto, P. (ed.) *Illuminating Social Life: Classical and Contemporary Theory Revisited.* Thousand Oaks, CA: Sage.

10. FAO, IFAD, UNICEF, WFP, & WHO. (2020). *The State of Food Security and Nutrition in the World 2020: Transforming Food Systems for Affordable Healthy Diets.* Rome.

11. IPBES. (2019). *Summary for Policymakers of the Global Assessment Report on Biodiversity and Ecosystem Services of the Intergovernmental Science-Policy Platform on Biodiversity and Ecosystem Services.* Bonn, Germany: IPBES secretariat.

12. Bowness, E., James, D., Desmarais, A.A., McIntyre, A., Robin, T., Dring, C., & Wittman, H. (2021). Risk and Responsibility in the Corporate Food Regime: Research Pathways Beyond the COVID-19 Crisis. *Studies in Political Economy, 101*(3): 245–263. <https://doi.org/10.1080/07078552.2020.1849986>.

13. McMichael, P. (2009). A Food Regime Analysis of the "World Food Crisis." *Agriculture and Human Values, 26*(4): 281–295. <https://doi.org/10.1007/s10460-009-9218-5>.

14 Moura, Renata. (2018). A cronologia da crise do diesel, do controle de preços de Dilma à greve dos caminhoneiros. *BBC News,* May 24. <https://www.bbc.com/portuguese/brasil-44239437>.

15. Fachin, P., & Petersen, P. (2018). Redes de agroecologia como uma alternativa à agricultura industrial. Entrevista especial com Paulo Petersen. *Instituto Humanitas Unisinos,* May 30. <http://www.ihu.unisinos.br/159-noticias/entrevistas/579458-redes-de-agroecologia-como-uma-alternativa-a-agricultura-industrial-entrevista-especial-com-paulo-petersen>.

16. Tendall, D.M., Joerin, J., Kopainsky, B., Edwards, P., Shreck, A., Le, Q.B., Kruetli, P., Grant, M., & Six, J. (2015). Food System Resilience: Defining the Concept. *Global Food Security, 6*(C): 17–23. <https://doi.org/10.1016/j.gfs.2015.08.001>.

17. Mendez, V.E., Bacon, C.M., Cohen, R., & Gliessman, S.R. (eds.). (2015). *Agroecology: A Transdisciplinary, Participatory and Action-oriented Approach.* Boca Raton: CRC Press. <https://www.researchgate.net/publication/282912317_Agroecology_a_transdisciplinary_participatory_and_action-oriented_approach>.

18. Wittman, H., Desmarais, Annette Aurélie, & Wiebe, N. (eds.). (2010). *Food Sovereignty: Reconnecting Food, Nature & Community.* Halifax, NS: Fernwood Publishing.

19. Wezel, A., Bellon, S., Doré, T., Francis, C., Vallod, D., & David, C. (2009). Agroecology as a Science, a Movement and a Practice: A Review. *Agronomy for Sustainable Development, 29*(4): 503–515.

20. Méndez, V.E., Bacon, C.M., Cohen, R., & Gliessman, S.R. (eds.). *Agroecology.*

21. James, D., Bowness, E., Robin, T., McIntyre, A., Dring, C., Desmarais, A. A., & Wittman, H. (2021). Dismantling and Rebuilding the Food System after COVID-19: Ten Principles for Redistribution and Regeneration. *Journal of Agriculture, Food Systems, and Community Development, 10*(2): 29–51. <https://www.foodsystemsjournal.org/index.php/fsj/article/view/923>.

22. Wright, E.O. (2010). *Envisioning Real Utopias.* London: Verso; Wright, E.O. (2007). Guidelines for Envisioning Real Utopias. *Soundings, 36*: 26–39.

23. Wright, E.O. (2006). Compass Points: Towards a Socialist Alternative. *New Left Review*, *41*: 110.

24. Wright, E.O. *Envisioning Real Utopias*: p. 1.

25. IFOAM. (n.d.). Participatory Guarantee Systems. <https://www.ifoam.bio/our-work/how/standards-certification/participatory-guarantee-systems>.

26. ILO. Employment in Agriculture (percent of total employment) (modeled ILO estimate). International Labour Organization, ILOSTAT database. <https://data.worldbank.org/indicator/SL.AGR.EMPL.ZS?locations=BR>.

27. Observatory of Economic Complexity (n.d.). Brazil. <https://oec.world/en/profile/country/bra/>.

28. Merry, F., & Soares-Filho, B. (2017). Will Intensification of Beef Production Deliver Conservation Outcomes in the Brazilian Amazon? *Elementa: Science of the Anthropocene*, *5*(24) <https://doi.org/10.1525/elementa.224>.

29. Lin, B.B., Chappell, M.J., Vandermeer, J., Smith, G., Quintero, E., Bezner-Kerr, R., ... Perfecto, I. (2011). Effects of Industrial Agriculture on Climate Change and the Mitigation Potential of Small-Scale Agro-Ecological Farms. *CABI Reviews: Perspectives in Agriculture, Veterinary Science, Nutrition and Natural Resources*, *6*(020). <https://doi.org/10.1079/PAVSNNR20116020>.

30. Gliessman, S. (2016). Transforming Food Systems with Agroecology. *Agroecology and Sustainable Food Systems*, *40*(3): 187–189. <https://doi.org/10.1080/21683565.2015.1130765>; Gliessman, S. (2015). *Agroecology: The Ecology of Sustainable Food Systems*. CRC Press.

31. Gliessman, S. Transforming Food Systems.

32. Sen, A. (1981). *Poverty and Famines*. Oxford: Oxford University Press; Sen, A. (1982). The Food Problem: Theory and Policy. *Third World Quarterly*, *4*(3): 447–459.

33. Sen, A. The Food Problem: p. 459.

34. Rockström, J., Steffen, W., Noone, K., Persson Å., Chapin, F.S., Lambin, E.F., ... Foley, J.A. (2009). A Safe Operating Space for Humanity. *Nature*, *461*(24): 472–475; Rockström, J., Steffen, W., Noone, K., Persson, Å., Chapin, F. S., Lambin, E. F., ... Foley, J. A. (2009). Planetary Boundaries: Exploring the Safe Operating Space for Humanity Johan. *Ecology & Society*, *14*(2): 32. <https://doi.org/10.1038/461472a>; Gordon, L.J., Bignet, V., Crona, B., Henriksson, P.J., Holt, T. van, Jonell, M., ... Queiroz, C. (2017). Rewiring Food Systems to Enhance Human Health and Biosphere Stewardship. *Environmental Research Letters*, *12*, 100201. <https://doi.org/10.1088/1748-9326/AA81DC>; Horton, R., & Lo, S. (2015). Planetary Health: A New Science for Exceptional Action. *The Lancet*, *386*(10007): 1921–1922. <https://doi.org/10.1016/S0140-6736(15)61038-8>.

Chapter 2

1. Malthus, T. (1798). *An Essay on the Principle of Population*. London: J. Johnson.

2. Evenson, R.E. (2005). Besting Malthus: The Green Revolution. *Proceedings of the American Philosophical Society*, *149*(4): 469–486.

3. Scoones, I., Smalley, R., Hall, R., & Tsikata, D. (2019). Narratives of Scarcity: Framing the Global Land Rush. *Geoforum*, *101*: 231–241. <https://doi.org/10.1016/j.geoforum.2018.06.006>.

4. Ortiz, R., Trethowan, R., Ferrara, G.O., Iwanaga, M., Dodds, J.H., Crouch, J.H., ... Braun, H.J. (2007). High Yield Potential, Shuttle Breeding, Genetic Diversity, and a New International Wheat Improvement Strategy. *Euphytica*, *157*(3): 365–384. <https://doi.org/10.1007/s10681-007-9375-9>.

5. Pingali, P.L. (2012). Green Revolution: Impacts, Limits, and the Path Ahead. *Proceedings of the National Academy of Sciences of the United States of America*, *109*(31): 12302. <https://doi.org/10.1073/pnas.0912953109>.

6. da Costa, M.B.B., Souza, M., Müller Júnior, V., Comin, J.J., & Lovato, P.E. (2017). Agroecology Development in Brazil between 1970 and 2015. *Agroecology and Sustainable Food Systems*, *41*(3–4): 276–295. <https://doi.org/10.1080/21683565.2017.1285382>.

7. Brazil was under a military dictatorship from 1964–1985.

8. Garrett, R.D., & Rausch, L.L. (2016). Green for Gold: Social and Ecological Tradeoffs Influencing the Sustainability of the Brazilian Soy Industry. *Journal of Peasant Studies*, *43*(2): 461–493. <https://doi.org/10.1080/03066150.2015.1010077>; OECD-FAO. (2015). Brazilian Agriculture: Prospects and Challenges. OECD-FAO *Agricultural Outlook 2015*. <https://www.oecd-ilibrary.org/agriculture-and-food/oecd-fao-agricultural-outlook-2015/brazilian-agriculture-prospects-and-challenges_agr_outlook-2015-5-en>.

9. Sencébé, Y., Pinton, F., & Cazella, A.A. (2020). On the Unequal Coexistence of Agrifood Systems in Brazil. *Review of Agricultural, Food and Environmental Studies, 101*: 191–212. <https://doi.org/10.1007/s41130-020-00099-8>.

10. Capellesso, A.J., Cazella, A.A., Schmitt Filho, A.L., Farley, J., & Martins, D.A. (2016). Economic and Environmental Impacts of Production Intensification in Agriculture: Comparing Transgenic, Conventional, and Agroecological Maize Crops. *Agroecology and Sustainable Food Systems*, *40*(3): 216. <https://doi.org/10.1080/21683565.2015.1128508>.

11. Derli, S., & Antonio, B.F. (1998). Soil Quality and Agricultural Sustainability in the Brazilian Cerrado. *Embrapa*. <https://www.embrapa.br/busca-de-publicacoes/-/publicacao/482346/soil-quality-and-agricultural-sustainability-in-the-brazilian-cerrado>; Rada, N. (2013). Assessing Brazil's Cerrado Agricultural Miracle. *Food Policy*, *38*(1): 146–155. <https://doi.org/10.1016/j.foodpol.2012.11.002>.

12. Carvalho, F.M.V., De Marco, P., & Ferreira, L.G. (2009). The Cerrado into Pieces: Habitat Fragmentation as a Function of Landscape Use in the Savannas of Central Brazil. *Biological Conservation*, *142*(7): 1392–1403. <https://www.sciencedirect.com/science/article/abs/pii/S000632070900072X>; Lin, B.B., Chappell, M.J., Vandermeer, J., Smith, G., Quintero, E., Bezner-Kerr, R., ... Perfecto, I. (2011). Effects of Industrial Agriculture on Climate Change and the Mitigation Potential of Small-Scale Agro-Ecological Farms. *CABI Reviews: Perspectives in Agriculture, Veterinary Science, Nutrition and Natural Resources*, *6*(020). <https://doi.org/10.1079/PAVSNNR20116020>; Brannstrom, C., Jepson, W., Filippi, A.M., Redo, D., Xu, Z., & Ganesh, S. (2008). Land Change in the Brazilian Savanna (Cerrado), 1986–2002: Comparative Analysis and Implications for Land-Use Policy. *Land Use Policy*, *25*(4): 579–595. <https://doi.org/10.1016/j.landusepol.2007.11.008>.

13. Tarlau, R. (2019). *Occupying Schools, Occupying Land: How the Landless Workers Movement Transformed Brazilian Education*. Oxford University Press; Carter, M. (2003). *The Origins of Brazil's Landless Rural Workers Movement (MST): The Natalino Episode in Rio Grande do Sul (1981–84). A Case of Ideal Interest Mobilization* (University of Oxford Centre for Brazilian Studies Working Paper Series). Oxford.

14. da Costa, Souza, et al. Agroecology Development in Brazil.

15. Lin, Chappell, et al. Effects of Industrial Agriculture on Climate Change.

16. Béné, C., Oosterveer, P., Lamotte, L., Brouwer, I.D., de Haan, S., Prager, S.D., ... Khoury, C. K. (2019). When Food Systems Meet Sustainability: Current Narratives and Implications for Actions. *World Development, 113*: 116–130. <https://doi.org/10.1016/j.worlddev.2018.08.011>.

17. FAO, IFAD, UNICEF, WFP, and WHO. (2020). *The State of Food Security and Nutrition in the World 2020: Transforming Food Systems for Affordable Healthy Diets*. Rome.

18. Bentham, J., Di Cesare, M., Bilano, V., Bixby, H., Zhou, B., Stevens, G.A., ... Cisneros, J.Z. (2017). Worldwide Trends in Body-Mass Index, Underweight, Overweight, and Obesity from 1975 to 2016: A Pooled Analysis of 2416 Population-Based Measurement Studies in 128.9 Million Children, Adolescents,

and Adults. *The Lancet, 390*(10113): 2627–2642. <https://doi.org/10.1016/S0140-6736(17)32129-3>.

19. Patel, R. (2008). *Stuffed and Starved: Markets, Power and the Hidden Battle for the World Food System* (1st Canadian Edition). HarperCollins.

20. FAO. (2019). *The State of Food and Agriculture 2019. Moving Forward on Food Loss and Waste Reduction.* Rome. <http://www.fao.org/3/ca6030en/ca6030en.pdf>; UNEP. (2021). UNEP Food Waste Index Report 2021. <https://www.unep.org/resources/report/unep-food-waste-index-report-2021>.

21. Mehrabi, Z., Gill, M., van Wijk, M., Herrero, M., & Ramankutty, N. (2020). Livestock Policy for Sustainable Development. *Nature Food, 1*(3): 160–165. <https://doi.org/10.1038/s43016-020-0042-9>.

22. FAO. (2020). *The State of Food and Agriculture 2020. Overcoming Water Challenges in Agriculture.* Rome. <https://doi.org/10.4060/cb1447en>.

23. Pennock, D. (2019). *Soil Erosion: The Greatest Challenge to Sustainable Soil Management.* Rome. FAO. <http://www.fao.org/3/ca4395en/ca4395en.pdf>.

24. Ripple, W.J., Wolf, C., Newsome, T.M., Barnard, P., & Moomaw, W.R. (2019). World Scientists' Warning of a Climate Emergency. *BioScience, 70*(1): 8–12. <https://doi.org/10.1093/biosci/biz088>; IPCC. (2019). *Climate Change and Land: Summary for Policymakers.* Geneva, Switzerland. <https://www.ipcc.ch/srccl/>; Ceballos, G., Ehrlich, P.R., Barnosky, A.D., García, A., Pringle, R.M., & Palmer, T.M. (2015). Accelerated Modern Human-Induced Species Losses: Entering the Sixth Mass Extinction. *Science Advances, 1*(5): 9–13. <https://doi.org/10.1126/sciadv.1400253>; Ceballos, G., & Ehrlich, P.R. (2018). The Misunderstood Sixth Mass Extinction. *Science, 360*(6393): 1080–1081.

25. Ramankutty, N., Mehrabi, Z., Waha, K., Jarvis, L., Kremen, C., Herrero, M., & Rieseberg, L.H. (2018). Trends in Global Agricultural Land Use: Implications for Environmental Health and Food Security. *Annual Review of Plant Biology, 69*(1): 789–815. <https://doi.org/10.1146/annurev-arplant-042817-040256>; Campbell, B.M., Beare, D.J., Bennett, E.M., Hall-Spencer, J.M., Ingram, J.S.I., Jaramillo, F., … Shindell, D. (2017). Agriculture Production as a Major Driver of the Earth System Exceeding Planetary Boundaries. *Ecology & Society, 22*(4): 8.

26. Campbell, Beare, et al. Agriculture Production.

27. Wallace, R. (2016). *Big Farms Make Big Flu: Dispatches on Influenza, Agribusiness, and the Nature of Science. Monthly Review*; IPES-Food. (2017). *Unravelling the Food–Health Nexus: Addressing Practices, Political Economy, and Power Relations to Build Healthier Food Systems.* The Global Alliance for the Future of Food and IPES-Food.

28. Hendrickson, M.K., Howard, P.H., Miller, E.M., & Constance, D.H. (2020). *The Food System: Concentration and Its Impacts*; IPES-Food. (2017). *Too Big to Feed: Exploring the Impacts of Mega-Mergers, Concentration, Concentration of Power in the Agri-Food Sector.* <http://www.ipes-food.org/_img/upload/files/Concentration_ExecSummary.pdf>.

29. IPES-Food. *Too Big to Feed.*

30. Van Boeckel, T.P., Pires, J., Silvester, R., Zhao, C., Song, J., Criscuolo, N.G., Gilbert, M., Sebastian Bonhoeffer, S. & Laxminarayan, R. (2019). Global Trends in Antimicrobial Resistance in Animals in Low- and Middle-Income Countries. *Science, 365*(6459). <https://science.sciencemag.org/content/365/6459/eaaw1944>; Van Boeckel, T.P., Glennon, E.E., Chen, D., Gilbert, M., Robinson, T.P., Grenfell, B.T., … Laxminarayan, R. (2017). Reducing Antimicrobial Use in Food Animals. *Science, 357*(6358): 1350–1352. <https://doi.org/10.1126/science.aao1495>; Silbergeld, E.K., Graham, J., & Price, L.B. (2008). Industrial Food Animal Production, Antimicrobial Resistance, and Human Health. *Annual Review of Public Health, 29*: 151–169. <https://doi.org/10.1146/annurev.publhealth.29.020907.090904>.

31. Nicholls, C.I., & Altieri, M.A. (1997). Conventional Agricultural Development Models and the Persistence of the Pesticide Treadmill in Latin America. *International Journal of Sustainable Development & World*

Ecology, 4(2): 93–111. <https://doi.org/10.1080/13504509709469946>; Bakker, L., Werf, W. van der, Tittonell, P., Wyckhuys, K., & Bianchi, F. (2020). Neonicotinoids in Global Agriculture: Evidence for a New Pesticide Treadmill? *Ecology and Society*, 25(3). <https://doi.org/10.5751/es-11814-250326>.

32. Mateo-Sagasta, J., Zadeh, S.M., Turral, H., & Burke, J. (2017). *Water Pollution from Agriculture: A Global Review. Executive Summary*. Rome: FAO Colombo, Sri Lanka: International Water Management Institute. CGIAR Research Program on Water, Land and Ecosystems. <http://www.fao.org/3/a-i7754e.pdf>.

33. Rigotto, R.M., Paixão e Vasconcelos, D., & Rocha, M.M. (2014). Pesticide Use in Brazil and Problems for Public Health. *Cadernos de Saude Publica*, 30(7): 1–3. <https://doi.org/10.1590/0102-311XPE020714>; Firpo de Souza Porto, M. (2018). The Tragic "Poison Package": Lessons for Brazilian Society and Public Health. *Cadernos de Saúde Pública*, 34(7): e00110118. <https://doi.org/10.1590/0102-311x00110118>; Dowler, C. (2020). Soya, Corn and Cotton Make Brazil World Leader for Hazardous Pesticides. *Unearthed*, February 2. <https://unearthed.greenpeace.org/2020/02/20/brazil-pesticides-soya-corn-cotton-hazardous-croplife/>.

34. Dowler, C. (2020). Revealed: The Pesticide Giants Making Billions on Toxic and Bee-Harming Chemicals. *Unearthed*, February 2. <https://unearthed.greenpeace.org/2020/02/20/pesticides-croplife-hazardous-bayer-syngenta-health-bees/>.

35. Dowler. Soya, Corn and Cotton.

36. FAO and WHO. (2019). *Detoxifying Agriculture and Health from Highly Hazardous Pesticides — A Call for Action*. Rome.

37. International Agency for Research on Cancer. (2016). *Q&A on Glyphosate*. <https://www.iarc.who.int/wp-content/uploads/2018/11/QA_Glyphosate.pdf>; Dowler. Revealed.

38. Tuncak, B. (2020). *Visit to Brazil: Report of the Special Rapporteur on the Implications for Human Rights of the Environmentally Sound Management and Disposal of Hazardous Substances and Wastes*. <https://terradedireitos.org.br/uploads/arquivos/A_HRC_45_12_Add.2-.pdf>.

39. McCoy, T. (2020). Agricultural Giant Brazil, a Growing Hazard: The Illegal Trade in Pesticides. *Washington Post*, February 9. <https://www.washingtonpost.com/world/the_americas/in-agricultural-giant-brazil-a-new-and-growing-hazard-the-illegal-trade-in-pesticides/2020/02/09/2c0b2f2e-30b3-11ea-a053-dc6d944ba776_story.html>.

40. Tuncak. *Visit to Brazil*.

41. Clarke, J.S. (2019). Brazil Pesticide Approvals Soar as Jair Bolsonaro Moves to Weaken Rules. *Unearthed*, June 12. <https://unearthed.greenpeace.org/2019/06/12/jair-bolsonaro-brazil-pesticides/>.

42. Firpo de Souza Porto. The Tragic "Poison Package."

43. Giovanaz, D. (2020). How Bolsonaro's Pro-Pesticide Policy Transfers Wealth Out of the Country. *Brasil de Fato*, December 16. <https://www.brasildefato.com.br/2020/12/16/how-bolsonaro-s-pro-pesticide-policy-transfers-wealth-outside-of-the-country>.

44. Bombardi, L.M. (2017). *Geografia do Uso de Agrotóxicos no Brasil e Conexões com a União Européia*. Sao Paulo: Laboratorio de Geografia Agraria: FFLCH-USP. <https://conexaoagua.mpf.mp.br/arquivos/agrotoxicos/05-larissa-bombardi-atlas-agrotoxico-2017.pdf>.

45. Clapp, J. (2018). Mega-Mergers on the Menu: Corporate Concentration and the Politics of Sustainability in the Global Food System. *Global Environmental Politics*, 18(2): 12–33. <https://direct.mit.edu/glep/article/18/2/12/14909/Mega-Mergers-on-the-Menu-Corporate-Concentration>; Clapp, J., & Fuchs, D. (2009). *Corporate Power in Global Agrifood Governance*. (J. Clapp & D. Fuchs, eds.). MIT Press; IPES-Food. *Too Big to Feed*; IPES-Food. (2016). *From Uniformity to Diversity: A Paradigm Shift from Industrial Agriculture to Diversified Agroecological Systems*. <http://www.ipes-food.org/_img/upload/files/UniformityToDiversity_ExecSummary.pdf>.

46. IPES-Food. *Too Big to Feed*: p. 71.
47. Campbell, H. (2009). Breaking New Ground in Food Regime Theory: Corporate Environmentalism, Ecological Feedbacks and the "Food from Somewhere" Regime? *Agriculture and Human Values, 26*(4): 309. <https://doi.org/10.1007/s10460-009-9215-8>.
48. Miles, A., DeLonge, M.S., & Carlisle, L. (2017). Triggering a Positive Research and Policy Feedback Cycle to Support a Transition to Agroecology and Sustainable Food Systems. *Agroecology and Sustainable Food Systems, 41*(7): 855–879. <https://doi.org/10.1080/21683565.2017.1331179>.
49. Leach, M., Nisbett, N., Cabral, L., Harris, J., Hossain, N., & Thompson, J. (2020). Food Politics and Development. *World Development, 134*, 105024. <https://doi.org/10.1016/j.worlddev.2020.105024>; Clapp, J., & Scott, C. (2018). The Global Environmental Politics of Food. *Global Environmental Politics, 18*(2): 1–11. <https://www.mitpressjournals.org/doi/full/10.1162/glep_a_00464>; Clapp. Mega-Mergers on the Menu.
50. Badgley, C., Moghtader, J., Quintero, E., Zakem, E., Chappell, M.J., Aviles-Vazquez, K., Samulon, A., & Perfecto, I. (2007). Organic Agriculture and the Global Food Supply. *Renewable Agriculture and Food Systems, 22*(2): 86–108; Davis, A.S., Hill, J.D., Chase, C. ., Johanns, A.M., & Liebman, M. (2012). Increasing Cropping System Diversity Balances Productivity, Profitability and Environmental Health. *PLoS ONE, 7*(10): e47149. <https://doi.org/10.1371/journal.pone.0047149>; Ricciardi, V., Mehrabi, Z., Wittman, H., James, D., Ramankutty, N. (2021). "Higher Yields and More Biodiversity on Smaller Farms." *Nature Sustainability, 4*: 651–657. <https://www.researchgate.net/publication/350400524_Higher_yields_and_more_biodiversity_on_smaller_farms>.
51. Wright, E.O. (2010). *Envisioning Real Utopias*. Verso.
52. ANA. (2018). *Carta Política do IV ENA*. Belo Horizonte. (Emphasis added). <http://enagroecologia.org.br/files/2019/03/carta_politica_web.pdf>.
53. IPES-Food. (2018). *Breaking Away from Industrial Food and Farming Systems: Seven Case Studies of Agroecological Transition*. <http://www.ipes-food.org/_img/upload/files/CS2_web.pdf>; Mier y Terán Giménez Cacho, M., Giraldo, O.F., Aldasoro, M., Morales, H., Ferguson, B.G., Rosset, P., ... Campos, C. (2018). Bringing Agroecology to Scale: Key Drivers and Emblematic Cases. *Agroecology and Sustainable Food Systems, 42*(6): 637–665. <https://doi.org/10.1080/21683565.2018.1443313>.
54. FAO. (2018). *The 10 Elements of Agroecology: Guiding the Transition to Sustainable Food and Agricultural Systems*. Rome.
55. HLPE. (2019). *Agroecological and Other Innovative Approaches for Sustainable Agriculture and Food Systems That Enhance Food Security and Nutrition*. Rome.
56. IPES-Food. *From Uniformity to Diversity*.

Chapter 3

1. Bové, J., and Dufour, F. (2002). Cited in McMichael, P. (2005). Global Development and the Corporate Food Regime. *Research in Rural Sociology and Development, 11*: 265.
2. Campbell, H. (2009). Breaking New Ground in Food Regime Theory: Corporate Environmentalism, Ecological Feedbacks and the "Food from Somewhere" Regime? *Agriculture and Human Values, 26*(4): 309. <https://doi.org/10.1007/s10460-009-9215-8>.
3. Gliessman, S. (2016). Transforming Food Systems with Agroecology. *Agroecology and Sustainable Food Systems, 40*(3): 187–189. <https://doi.org/10.1080/21683565.2015.1130765>.
4. Rede Ecovida. (n.d.). Sobre. <http://ecovida.org.br/sobre/>. (Authors' translation.)
5. ANA. (2019). Agricultores da Borborema debatem Reforma da Previdência durante Evento de

Planejamento. Articulação Nacional de Agroecologia. April 1. <https://agroecologia.org.br/2019/04/01/agricultores-da-borborema-debatem-reforma-da-previdencia-durante-evento-de-planejamento/>.

6. Veras Soares, F., Nehring, R., Battaglin Schwengber, R., Guimarães Rodrigues, C., Lambais, G., Silva Balaban, D., ... Galante, A. (2013). *Structured Demand and Smallholder Farmers in Brazil: The Case of PAA and PNAE*. Brasilia, DF.

7. Guerra, J., Blesh, J., Schmitt Filho, A.L., & Wittman, H. (2017). Pathways to Agroecological Management Through Mediated Markets in Santa Catarina, Brazil. *Elementa*, 5: 67. <https://doi.org/10.1525/elementa.248>.

8. Guerra, Blesh, et al. Pathways to Agroecological Management; Valencia, V., Wittman, H., & Blesh, J. (2019). Structuring Markets for Resilient Farming Systems. *Agronomy for Sustainable Development*, 39(25).

9. Associação dos Agricultores Ecológicos das Encostas da Serra Geral (Association of Ecological Farmers of the Encostas da Serra Geral).

10. Wallace, R. (2016). *Big Farms Make Big Flu: Dispatches on Influenza, Agribusiness, and the Nature of Science*. NYU Press.

11. Reis, M.S; Peroni, N; Mariot, A; Steenbock, W.; Filippon, S.; Silva, C.V. Mantovani, A. (2010). Uso Sustentável E Domesticação De Espécies Da Floresta Ombrófila Mista. In Ming, L.C.; Amorozo, M.C.M.; Kffuri, C.W. (Orgs.), *Agrobiodiversidade No Brasil: Experiências E Caminhos Da Pesquisa*. Recife: Nupeea, p. 183–214.

12. Mantovani, A; Da Costa, N.C.F. (2018). Situação Atual E Conservação Das Florestas Com Araucária. In Anais 3º Seminário Sul-brasileiro Sobre A Sustentabilidade Da Araucária. *Passo Fundo*, 23–25 may. <http://www.Upf.Br/Araucaria/Download>.

13. Peters, C.M. Gentry, A.H. Mendelsohn, R.O. (1989). Valuation of the Amazon Rainforest. *Nature*, 339: 645-656.

14. Planalto Serrano Catarinense is composed of eighteen municipalities that make up the Association of Municipalities of Serra Catarinense and cover a total area of 16,085 square kilometres, which represents 16.9 percent of Santa Catarina's area.

15. Magnanti, N.J.; Sartori, S. (2011). Sistematização do Território Serra Catarinense. Termo de referência do Projeto MA 429. Federation of Bodies for Social and Educational Assistance, FASE.

16. Diegues, A.C; Arruda, R.S.V. (2001). *Saberes Tradicionais E Biodiversidade No Brasil*. Brasília: Ministry of the Environment, São Paulo: USP; Bensusan, N. (2006). Conservação Da Biodiversidade Em Áreas Protegidas. Editora Fgv, 176p; Vieira da Silva, C.A. (2013). (In)visibilidade de uma atividade praticada por muitos: o extrativismo e os canais de comercialização de pinhão em São Francisco de Paula, RS. Doctoral thesis, Programa de Pós-Graduação em Desenvolvimento Rural/UFRGS,

17. Magnanti, N.J. (2016) A importância social e econômica do pinhão na Serra Catarinense. In Peixer, Z. & Carraro, J.L. (eds.), *Povos do campo, educação e natureza*. Lages (SC): Grafine: p. 188.

18. Mantovani, A; Morellato, L.P.C.; Reis, M.S. (2004). Fenologia reprodutiva e produção de sementes em Araucária angustifólia. *Revista Brasileira de Botânica*, 27(4): 787–796.

19. EPAGRI / CEPA. (2018). *Síntese anual da agricultura de Santa Catarina 2016–2017*. Secretariat of Agriculture and Fisheries. <https://publicacoes.epagri.sc.gov.br/SAA/article/view/521>.

20. Pinto, L.F.G., Guidotti De Faria, V., Sparovek, G., Reydon, B.P., Ramos, C.A., Siqueira, G.P., ... Couto, M. (2020). *Quem São Os Poucos Donos Das Terras Agrícolas No Brasil - O Mapa Da Desigualdade. Sustentabilidade em Debate*. <https://www.imaflora.org/public/media/biblioteca/1588006460-sustentabilidade_terras_agricolas.pdf>.

21. Wittman, H. (2009). Reframing Agrarian Citizenship: Land, Life and power in Brazil. *Journal of Rural*

Studies, 25: 120–130. <https://doi.org/10.1016/j.jrurstud.2008.07.002>.

22. Wittman. Reframing Agrarian Citizenship.

2w. Adriano, J. (2020). MST em Santa Catarina comemora 35 anos com atos de solidariedade. *MST* May 27. <https://mst.org.br/2020/05/27/mst-em-santa-catarina-comemora-35-anos-com-atos-de-solidariedade/>.

24. Tarlau, R. (2019). *Occupying Schools, Occupying Land: How the Landless Workers Movement Transformed Brazilian Education.* Oxford University Press; Meek, D. (2015). Learning as Territoriality: The Political Ecology of Education int Brazilian Landless Workers' Movement. *Journal of Peasant Studies, 42*(6): 1179–1200.

Chapter 4

1. Foster, J.B., Clark, B., & York, R. (2011). *The Ecological Rift: Capitalism's War on the Earth.* NYU Press.

2. Schneider, M., & McMichael, P. (2010). Deepening, and Repairing, the Metabolic Rift. *Journal of Peasant Studies, 37*(3): 461–484. <https://doi.org/10.1080/03066150.2010.494371>.

3. De Tavernier, J. (2012). Food Citizenship: Is There a Duty for Responsible Consumption? *Journal of Agricultural and Environmental Ethics, 25*(6): 895–907.

4. Bové, J., and Dufour, F. (2002), cited in McMichael, P. (2005). Global Development and the Corporate Food Regime. *Research in Rural Sociology and Development, 11*: 265–299.

5. Acolhida na Colônia. (n.d.). *Objetivos.* <https://acolhida.com.br/sobre/objetivos/>.

6. Acolhida na Colônia. *Objetivos.*

7. Gliessman, S. (2016). Transforming Food Systems with Agroecology. *Agroecology and Sustainable Food Systems, 40*(3): 187–189. <https://doi.org/10.1080/21683565.2015.1130765>.

8. Jose, S. (2009). Agroforestry for Ecosystem Services and Environmental Benefits: An Overview. *Agroforestry Systems, 76*(1): 1–10.

9. LACAF/UFSC. (n.d.) Células de Consumidores Responsáveis. <https://lacaf.paginas.ufsc.br/celulas-de-consumidores-responsaveis/>.

10. Vidgen, H.A., & Gallegos, D. (2014). Defining Food Literacy and Its Components. *Appetite, 76*: 50–59. <https://doi.org/10.1016/j.appet.2014.01.010>.

11. Escosteguy, I., Rover, O., Romão, A., & Morelli, N. (2018). Networks of Agrifood Citizenship: The Case of Responsible Consumption Cells in Florianópolis-SC. *Cadernos de Agroecologia, 13*(1).

12. You can find more information about the Responsible Consumer Cells here. <https://celulasconsumo.ufsc.br/>.

Chapter 5

1. Gliessman, S. (2016). Transforming Food Systems with Agroecology. *Agroecology and Sustainable Food Systems, 40*(3):187–89. <https://doi.org/10.1080/21683565.2015.1130765>.

2. Gliessman. Transforming Food Systems.

3. de Molina, M.G. (2013). Agroecology and Politics. How to Get Sustainability? About the Necessity for a Political Agroecology, *Agroecology and Sustainable Food Systems, 37*(1): 45–59. <DOI: 10.1080/10440046.2012.705810>.

4. Bowness, E., Nicklay, J., Liebman, A., Cadieux, V., and Blumberg, R. (2020). "Navigating Urban Agroecology with the Social Sciences." In Egerer, M., & Cohen, H. (eds.), *Interdisciplinary Research in Urban Agroecology.* CRC Press.

5. White, B. (2020). *Agriculture and the Generation Problem.* Halifax: Fernwood Publishing.

6. IBGE. (2017). *Resultados definitivos: Produtores.* <https://censoagro2017.ibge.gov.br/templates/censo_agro/resultadosagro/produtores.html>.

7. Hebinck, P. (2018). De-/re-agrarianisation: Global Perspectives. *Journal of Rural Studies*, 61(May): 227–235. <https://doi.org/10.1016/j.jrurstud.2018.04.010>.

8. Blay-Palmer, A., Santini, G., Dubbeling, M., Renting, H., Taguchi, M., & Giordano, T. (2018). Validating the City Region Food System Approach: Enacting Inclusive, Transformational City Region Food Systems. *Sustainability*, *10*(5): 1680.

9. HLPE. (2021). Promoting Youth Engagement and Employment in Agriculture and Food Systems. <http://www.fao.org/3/cb5463en/cb5463en.pdf>.

10. Waltz, A. (2016). The Women Who Feed Us: Gender Empowerment (or Lack Thereof) in Rural Southern Brazil. *Journal of Rural Studies*, *47*(A): 31–40. <https://doi.org/10.1016/j.jrurstud.2016.07.009>.

11. ANA. (2018). *Carta Política do IV ENA.* Belo Horizonte. <http://enagroecologia.org.br/files/2019/03/carta_politica_web.pdf>.

12. MMC. (n.d.). "História." MMC. <https://www.mmcbrasil.com.br/site/node/44>.

13. Bezner-Kerr, R. (2020). Towards a Feminist Reparative Agroecology. *Farming Matters. Agroecology and Feminism: Transforming Our Economy and Society*, *1*: 31.

14. ANA. *Carta Política do IV ENA.*

15. Hidalgo, F.D., Naidu, S., Nichter, S., & Richardson, N. (2010). Economic Determinants of Land Invasions. *Review of Economics and Statistics*, *92*(3): 505–523; Johnson, H.B. (1987). Portuguese Settlement, 1500–1580. In L. Bethell (ed.), *Colonial Brazil* (p. 1–39). Cambridge, UK: Cambridge University Press.

16. Begotti, R.A., & Peres, C.A. (2020). Rapidly Escalating Threats to the Biodiversity and Ethnocultural Capital of Brazilian Indigenous Lands. *Land Use Policy*, *96*(July): 104694. <https://doi.org/10.1016/j.landusepol.2020.104694>; Sparovek, G., Reydon, B.P., Guedes Pinto, L.F., Faria, V., de Freitas, F.L.M., Azevedo-Ramos, C., … Ribeiro, V. (2019). Who Owns Brazilian Lands? *Land Use Policy*, *87*: 104062. <https://doi.org/10.1016/j.landusepol.2019.104062>.

17. The Intercept Brasil. (2017). "Bolsonaro faz discurso de ódio no Clube Hebraica." YouTube video. 1:05, April 5. <https://www.youtube.com/watch?v=zSTdTjsio5g>.

18. CIMI. (2018). *Violência contra os Povos Indígenas no Brasil – Dados de 2018.* <https://cimi.org.br/wp-content/uploads/2019/09/relatorio-violencia-contra-os-povos-indigenas-brasil-2018.pdf>.

19. Zuker, F. (2020). Indigenous Land Intrusions Help Drive Higher Virus Death Toll in the Amazon. *Reuters*, August 14. <https://www.reuters.com/article/us-health-coronavirus-brazil-amazon-anal-idUSKCN25A2BX>.

20. ANA. (2019). Carta Terra e Território propõe barrar retrocessos e unir pauta agrária e ambiental. Articulação Nacional de Agroecologia. <https://agroecologia.org.br/2019/06/10/carta-terra-e-territorio-propoe-barrar-retrocessos-e-unir-pauta-agraria-e-ambiental/>.

21. ANA. (2018). Povos Indígenas demarcam território no IV ENA. Articulação Nacional de Agroecologia, June 3. <https://agroecologia.org.br/2018/06/03/povos-indigenas-demarcam-territorio-no-iv-ena/>.

22. de Castro, I.R.R. (2019). A extinção do conselho nacional de segurança alimentar e nutricional e a agenda de alimentação e nutrição. *Cadernos de Saude Publica*, *35*(2): 1–4. <https://doi.org/10.1590/0102-311x00009919>.

23. Sonnino, R., Torres, C.L., & Schneider, S. (2014). Reflexive Governance for Food Security: The Example of School Feeding in Brazil. *Journal of Rural Studies*, *36*: 1–12. <https://doi.org/10.1016/j.jrurstud.2014.06.003>.

24. Pogrebinschi, T., & Samuels, D. (2014). The Impact of Participatory Democracy: Evidence from Brazil's National Public Policy Conferences. *Comparative Politics*, *46*(3): 313–332. <https://doi.org/10.5129/001041514810943045>.

25. Recine, E., Fagundes, A., Silva, B.L., Garcia, G.S., Ribeiro, R. De C.L., & Gabriel, C.G. (2020). Reflections on the Extinction of the National Council for Food and Nutrition Security and the Confrontation of COVID-19 in Brazil. *Revista de Nutrição, 33*: e200176. <https://doi.org/10.1590/1678-9865202033e200176>.

26. Rajão, R., Soares-Filho, B., Nunes, F., Börner, J., Machado, L., Assis, D., Oliveira, A., Pinto, L., Ribeiro, V., Rausch, L., Gibbs, H., & Figueira, D. (2020). The Rotten Apples of Brazil's Agribusiness. *Science, 369*(6501): 246–248. <https://doi.org/10.1126/science.aba6646>.

27. Santarelli, M., David, G., Burity, V., & Rocha, N.C. (2019). *Informe Dhana 2019: Autoritarismo, negação de direitos e fome.* Brasília: FIAN Brasil.

28. Wittman, Hannah. (2015). "From Protest to Policy: The Challenges of Institutionalizing Food Sovereignty." *Canadian Food Studies/La Revue canadienne des études sur l'alimentation, 2*(2): 174–182.

29. ANA. *Carta Política do IV ENA.*

30. van den Berg, L., Goris, M.B., Behagel, J.H., Verschoor, G., Turnhout, E., Botelho, M.I.V., & Silva Lopes, I. (2019). Agroecological Peasant Territories: Resistance and Existence in the Struggle for Emancipation in Brazil. *Journal of Peasant Studies, 48*(3): 658–679. <https://doi.org/10.1080/03066150.2019.168300 1>; Andrade, D. (2019). Populism from Above and Below: The Path to Regression in Brazil. *Journal of Peasant Studies, 47*(7): 1470–1496. <https://doi.org/10.1080/03066150.2019.1680542>; Magalhães, F. (2019). Post-Democracy Reset: Brazil's Putschist Fix in Socio-Spatial Perspective. *South Atlantic Quarterly, 18*(2): 401–419. <https://doi.org/10.1215/00382876-7381218>.

31. Wright, E. O. (2007). Guidelines for Envisioning Real Utopias. *Soundings, 36*: 26–39.

32. Gliessman. Transforming Food Systems.

33. Martínez-Torres, M.E., & Rosset, P. (2014). Diálogo De Saberes in La Vía Campesina: Food Sovereignty and Agroecology. *Journal of Peasant Studies, 41*(6): 1–20. <https://doi.org/10.1080/03066150.2013.87 2632>.

DISCUSSION QUESTIONS

CHAPTER 1

1. How would you define an industrial food system in one sentence? What is an agroecological food system? What are their key differences?
2. In your view, what would transitioning from the industrial food system to agroecological food systems entail? What would we gain from such a transition?
3. What makes Brazil's engagement with agroecology unique? What lessons can Brazilian agroecology teach us?

CHAPTER 2

1. Describe the following:
   - rationalization
   - McDonaldization
   - Green Revolution.
2. Do you think that the industrial food system can feed the world sustainably? Why or why not?
3. Name some of the negative externalities associated with the industrial food system. Discuss the different categories that these costs fall into (e.g., health, environmental, economic, social).
4. Reflecting on or prioritizing issues and topics related to food systems can sometimes demonstrate what we value in our lives. Which of the costs listed above do you think most need to be addressed? Why?

CHAPTER 3

1. What are the differences between third-party and participatory forms of certification?
2. What do you think should be the role of governments in supporting agroecology? Do

you know of any examples of government programs or policies that support organic or agroecological farmers where you live?

3. What are some examples of barriers or challenges that farmers face in transitioning toward agroecological management? What are some of the benefits or opportunities available to farmers?

4. Are any of these barriers or benefits specific to different types of farms?

5. What is land reform? Do you think land occupations are an "acceptable" strategy for pursuing agroecological transitions? Why or why not?

CHAPTER 4

1. In your own words, how would you describe (a) the metabolic rift? (b) the knowledge rift?

2. Using some of the concepts and examples from this chapter, what are some ways that agroecology can connect urban and rural people and places and build new relationships?

3. Think about the different market arrangements discussed in this chapter. Which of these are present or most prevalent in your area? How does privilege shape who does and does not have access to organic or agroecological foods in your community?

CHAPTER 5

1. What makes agroecology and food systems "political"?

2. How are food-systems struggles shaped by age, gender, race, and Indigeneity (as well as other aspects of social identities, and their intersections)?

3. What are the political and economic limitations in Brazil that threaten agroecological transitions?

4. What are some examples of agroecological "real utopias" that you have encountered in your life, and what aspects make them strong examples? What are their stated principles or goals?

5. Do you think an agroecological food system is possible? What would it look like where you live?

INDEX

ABOUT THE AUTHORS

DANA JAMES is a critical geographer, political ecologist, and Vanier Scholar, Public Scholar, and PhD Candidate at the Centre for Sustainable Food Systems and the Institute for Resources, Environment and Sustainability at UBC. Dana's research interests include agroecology, food and land sovereignty, and environmental and climate justice.

EVAN BOWNESS is an environmental sociologist, urban political ecologist, and postdoctoral fellow at the Food and Agriculture Institute at the University of the Fraser Valley. He holds a PhD from the Institute for Resources, Environment and Sustainability at UBC. Evan studies urban agroecology, emerging agricultural technologies, and the corporate food regime.

The authors contributed equally to this book.